VALUE CRISIS

The Happy Family through Family Communion

Sukhi Parivaar

Value Crisis

The Happy Family through Family Communion

Sukhi Parivaar

Soodursun Jugessur
Pro-Chancellor and Chairman, University of Mauritius
Chairman, UOM Trust
Chairman, Mauritius Research Council
Founder Chairman, Mauritius Academy of Science and Technology

Allied Publishers Pvt. Ltd.
New Delhi • Mumbai • Kolkata • Lucknow • Chennai
Nagpur • Bangalore • Hyderabad • Ahmedabad

ALLIED PUBLISHERS PRIVATE LIMITED

1/13-14 Asaf Ali Road, **New Delhi**–110002
Ph.: 011-23239001 • E-mail: delhi.books@alliedpublishers.com

47/9 Prag Narain Road, Near Kalyan Bhawan, **Lucknow**–226001
Ph.: 0522-2209942 • E-mail: lko.books@alliedpublishers.com

17 Chittaranjan Avenue, **Kolkata**–700072
Ph.: 033-22129618 • E-mail: cal.books@alliedpublishers.com

15 J.N. Heredia Marg, Ballard Estate, **Mumbai**–400001
Ph.: 022-42126969 • E-mail: mumbai.books@alliedpublishers.com

60 Shiv Sunder Apartments (Ground Floor), Central Bazar Road,
Bajaj Nagar, **Nagpur**–440010
Ph.: 0712-2234210 • E-mail: ngp.books@alliedpublishers.com

F-1 Sun House (First Floor), C.G. Road, Navrangpura,
Ellisbridge P.O., **Ahmedabad**–380006
Ph.: 079-26465916 • E-mail: ahmbd.books@alliedpublishers.com

751 Anna Salai, **Chennai**–600002
Ph.: 044-28523938 • E-mail: chennai.books@alliedpublishers.com

5th Main Road, Gandhinagar, **Bangalore**–560009
Ph.: 080-22262081 • E-mail: bngl.books@alliedpublishers.com

3-2-844/6 & 7 Kachiguda Station Road, **Hyderabad**–500027
Ph.: 040-24619079 • E-mail: hyd.books@alliedpublishers.com

Website: www.alliedpublishers.com

ISBN: 978-81-8424-842-5

Published by Sunil Sachdev and printed by Ravi Sachdev at
Allied Publishers Pvt. Ltd. (Printing Division),
A-104 Mayapuri Phase II, New Delhi-110064

Invocation

Lord, enable us to protect one another!
Lord, enable us to share what we have with one another!
Lord, enable us to combine our physical strength to achieve great tasks!
Lord, enable us to put our heads together to find solutions to our problems!
So that, Oh Lord, there be no misunderstanding amongst us!

'May all people be happy! May all be healthy!
May we see to the welfare of all,
so that none may suffer!'

Foreword

Professor Soodursun Jugessur's book entitled "Value Crisis, Sukhi Parivaar or the Happy Family, through Family Communion' is most timely and pertinent since families across the globe are having to grapple with a number of issues and often struggle to find a way to hold their families together in peace and happiness. The multiplicity of crises such as the global financial crisis, the climate change crisis, the food crisis and persistent inequitable commerce have ripple effects on the sustainability of livelihoods and by extension on family living and lifestyles.

Families do not constitute monolithic, homogeneous blocks. Families of the 21st century come in all forms, types and sizes. Divorce, remarriage, parenting out of wedlock and a host of other variables have turned the common nuclear families into diverse kinds of units. The last several decades have witnessed nothing short of a revolution in marriage and family relationships. The rapidly evolving cultural, social and economic matrix pose new challenges to families—be they from the upper class, middle or working class. As members of families struggle to chart their trajectories in the midst of all kinds of uncertainties, they often get trapped in their own 'silences'. The latter can have deleterious effects on the individual. This is perhaps why Professor Jugessur's proposed 'Sukhi Parivaar or the Happy Family' program becomes relevant. The author notes:

> "This program would have taught the people to speak the truth without fear, to express themselves freely and thus contribute to developing trust, mutual love and understanding and the spirit of

> solidarity." Elaborating on his concept of 'Sukhi Parivaar', Professor Jugessur makes it clear that communication and dialogue are central to the spirit of family communion.

The book takes us through an analysis of how values and the spirit of sharing can be enhanced. In a world which is marked by 'isms' such as terrorism, individualism, managerialism, postfordism and neoliberalism, Prof Jugessur shows us that there is the need for another kind of ism—spiritualism. Drawing from a number of stories, poems, proverbs and quoting from a variety of sources, the author highlights how important it is to connect and reconnect with ourselves and our loved ones. The sea of modernity in which we swim and battle on an everyday basis often makes us forget the little, simple and beautiful things of life. Modernization can bring in its wake a number of opportunities and positive changes but it can also be detrimental to happy and secure living. Modernization can also increase the risk of human beings' erring. Such errings often accompanied by an erosion of values make the 'Sukhi Parivaar/Happy Family' program even more essential. If such a program and what Professor Jugessur is proposing can assist in preventing further violence, decay, selfishness, aggressive competition, individualism, obscene inequality, ostentation and can contribute to making the world a better, healthier, happier and a safer place for each and all, then every effort should be made to read this book and propagate the program. I have no doubt that the book will make useful and interesting reading for a wide array of people from diverse walks of life.

Professor Sheila Bunwaree
Chair of Gender and Development Studies
Faculty of Social Science and Humanities
University of Mauritius Reduit, Mauritius

Acknowledgements

The author is grateful to all those who have contributed to the Sukhi Parivaar or Happy Family movement, for their useful suggestions, and for the time and resources they have devoted to making this movement effect some changes in people's lives and get its local and international recognition. It is through the stewardship of this movement that I have found the need to develop the ideas and express them in this book for the benefit of mankind.

In a world where people have no time for others, and where voluntary participation for a social cause is rare, I am very grateful to the members of the executive committee, past and present, of Sukhi Parivaar for their selfless support. In its early days the commitment of Ms. Nina Gopaul, the Chairperson of Mosaic, has been exemplary. Even now, when her health has not allowed her to participate actively, she keeps enquiring after the welfare of the movement.

Various social and religious organizations, as well as concerned Ministries and their Departments in the Government have given a hand in promoting the concepts outlined in this book, and I am indebted to them all. I cannot forget Mr. Claudio Caldarone, the last UN Resident Coordinator and Resident Representative in Mauritius for his encouragement in promoting this concept. Recently, the National Women's Council has been instrumental in our seminars and workshops, and lately the Elderly People's Council.

Senior Professor Dr. K. Srinivasa Rao, Director (Hon) of the Srinivasa Ramanujan Academy in Chennai, has been of very great assistance in contacting the

Publisher and Mr. Armoogum Parsuraman, past Minister of Education and Director in UNESCO, has also been very helpful in establishing necessary contacts. I am thankful to them also.

I am especially grateful to Mr. Haymant Ramgobin, Mr. Lindsay Morvan, Ms. Vimi Dookhun, Mr. Philip Tse Rai Wai, Mr. Vijaye Kumar Beeharry, Mr. Premchand Jeetun, Dr. Ibrahim Koodorut, Dr. Ravhee Bholah, Mr. Shyam Hurbans, Mr. Dewanand Bhunjun, Mr. Kris Gunnoo, Mr. Parmanad Ramlakhan, Mr. Boopen Dobah, Mr. V. Jaunkeypersad, Mr. Asrani Gopaul, Mr. Riad Sultan, and Mrs. Lakshmi Gunessee, Ms. Sultana Kootbally, Ms. Jacqueline Darsoniah and Ms. Nivedita Seewoogobin, for their invaluable support. If I have missed out any names, I am thankful to them also.

Preface

Why another book on family issues and family happiness when the literature is flooded by umpteen writings on the topic? The search for happiness is an eternal pursuit of humankind. But, in this process, is the power of universal values and family communion properly grasped? Communion is when the doors of our minds and hearts are open to those around, and we feel united in them, sharing the same pleasures and pains that make life.

During my travels and prolonged stays in various parts of the world in the pursuit of acquiring scientific knowledge and promoting the same, I had the opportunity to mix and exchange views on ways to improve living in environments that were often hostile both in terms of natural settings and human frailties. I saw the gradual destruction of eternal human values led by the spirit of strife caused by inequities, exploitation of one group by another dominant one based on a visible lack of value-based basic education that is centered around the needs of colonizers, past and present, a consumerist culture promoted by development pundits, and increased distrust even within the primary cell, the family. Individualism was being extolled to the detriment of the spirit of sharing and fellow feeling. Ruthless competition had replaced the spirit of cooperation and solidarity based on empathy and compassion.

Back home in Mauritius I plunged headlong in science-based social advancement of the people, remembering that as human beings we have the same origins and the same destiny on a fragile planet. But the hostile environment nurtured by years of mutual distrust based on false notions of superiority of race, color and creed, and promoted by the powers around could not allow me to stay without voicing my opinion. This gave rise to the genesis of this book and the setting up of an NGO, the Sukhi Parivaar or the Happy Family. No sooner than this organization was formed and its program exposed, that the world was struck by the awareness of havocs of global warming and global financial crisis! These are now forcing countries and peoples to review their ways of living in the face of major economies going near bankrupt and hundreds of thousands of workers being ruthlessly laid off. Our civilization is under the microscope, and we are wondering why these had to happen!

Daily we are flooded with news of accounts of strife, violence within families and in the society, increase in drug and alcohol abuse, delinquency of children, unethical dealings of people and corporations, wars and a host of unhappy events. We tend to reconcile ourselves as helpless persons or accuse others for what happens, but rarely do we ask ourselves whether we are ourselves assuming our primary roles. Individual and group actions determine the events that we witness. What should then be our position and the way forward? The book outlines a basic strategy for enabling a change in the way we live and act so as to promote a better world.

In a body the primary structure is made of the biological cell, and its healthy growth determines the nature of the body. In a similar way, the world is made up of nations, and the nations of people grouped in families. If we can promote the healthy growth of the people and their families in their physical, psychological, material and spiritual development, we can ensure a better individual, a better nation and hence a better world. We seem to be making an appearance garbed in fashionable costumes when our inside is slowly dying due to a cancer that has attacked the primary cell. The gloss and glamour will not make us any happier for multiple forms of ailments are overpowering us.

So we have to start right at the very roots. That is why caring for the individual, tackling family issues and promoting family happiness are so important to ensure local and global peace and harmony. Our future lies in the way we live at present, and if we can, through family education, enable the members to be more responsible and take charge of their own development in consonance with global needs, we can ensure sustainability of this development. The current issues of global warming and its impacts on our lives are elements that we cannot ignore, and we have to educate and alert people so that they take necessary precautions. Changing mindsets is not easy and we have to start within the family where the primary seeds of development are nurtured.

Our present civilization has been led by science and technology that have enhanced our horizons, prolonged our life, reduced drudgery and brought more material comforts. While the standard of living has increased, one wonders whether the quality of life has really improved. Life is a mixture of both the material and the spiritual, and happiness a state where both these elements are in a balanced harmony within society. The pursuit of happiness is an individual and collective right. Our present bias on a career-oriented education is not giving proper results as little stress is currently laid on universal values that enrich life. It has to be supplemented by these universal values, and this should start within the family, the first nursery, through regular contacts and dialogues. When the roots are properly nurtured, the tree is most likely to be strong and healthy, and bear the fruits as desired.

The way we are presently embracing development has led to continual strife amongst communities and nations, mistrust and violence within families, increased delinquency and drug addiction, corruption at high levels, greed within business corporations, overconsumption of limited natural resources and global warming and global financial crisis. In parallel there is a gradual disruption of the family bonds, leading to a marked sense of individualism and selfishness. Moreover, old family values of mutual support and consideration for the elderly are fast disappearing. There is urgent need to go back to basics, revise our vision of development, and ensure universal values of empathy, compassion, sharing, thrift, trust, love and harmony, essential ingredients in our healthy living in tune with nature. These values are common to all religions, and stress must be placed on promoting them rather than on the theological differences that divide us. The Sukhi Parivaar program through its stress on family communion, highlights and promotes these values, starting from the role of individuals in families, and actions as a group. It caters for the holistic material, spiritual and social development.

People go astray and family bonds break when we do not take time to share our life, dialogue with members of the family regularly, and establish lasting healthy relationships that ensure harmony, peace and solidarity at home. We must understand that higher earnings and material comfort are important, but less important than the peace, harmony and love we share in our family. If we are happy at home, we can do better at work, be more efficient and productive. This is the basis for healthy development.

The book is meant to educate people on the need to change our lifestyles by first taking stock of what presently exists, and effecting the necessary and possible changes within our families. Understanding why we behave in a particular way and why we go for the easy life that our development brings are prerequisites for taking the necessary measures to avoid pitfalls. All these aspects are covered in the chapters that follow. It is full of examples to learn from. Competition in daily life, the post-industrial revolution, stages of human development, proper parenting, character building, pitfalls, roles of socio-cultural and religious organizations, some introspective interrogations, humanity's risky future, the quest for happiness, and bringing family values back, form the main chapters.

Understandably we tend to embrace life as it comes and make full use of the possibilities offered by our technological civilization. This is normal. But what is not normal is when our children no more listen to us and take to life patterns that are self-destructive: alcohol, drugs, excessive sex, violence, greed and consumerism with a perverted sense of individualism. We then suffer in silence and blame others for what is happening. That is why feasible and timely precautionary measures are essential, and the Sukhi Parivaar program brings these in our control. An ideal society may not be possible within our lifetime, but sincere efforts to reach such a state are within our means. And those who have practiced the program have recorded positive results.

The success of this program is directly proportional to the rate and amount of promotional campaign we can muster to educate the stakeholders. At the level of the families it does not require extra material and financial resources. It only requires a commitment to take time from our busy schedules to devote to dialogue within the family. Once we reach a certain level of awareness, our duty towards ourselves and our family and society propels us forward. Parents have a unique role in the process. They have to transform themselves first, and give the right signal to their children.

Sacrifice is the beginning of any positive and healthy development.

Soodursun Jugessur

Contents

Chapter I

Introduction

'The whole world is an extended family.'

—Vedas

Whenever I see something wrong happening around, whether as portrayed on the media or in the society, I feel that things would have been different if the Sukhi Parivaar or the Happy Family program had been followed, and people would have grasped the power of family communion. This program would have taught the people to speak the truth without fear, to express themselves freely and thus contribute to developing trust, mutual love and understanding, and the spirit of solidarity. In essence, the program requires that the members of a family communicate daily if possible, in a spirit of family communion, where open dialogue and recounting the day's events, sharing the joys, sorrows, achievements, disappointments, successes and failures, become a routine. Such dialogues develop the trust, love and family bonds that enable peace, harmony and mutual understanding within the fold. These are prerequisites for happiness within the family. And as the society is made of families, the entire society can be a living expression of such happiness if all families follow the program.

Most problems arise because, since childhood, people have not been trained to share their thoughts and feelings openly in an atmosphere of trust and mutual support. Whenever they hide their feelings and refrain from speaking their minds, they contribute to creating misunderstanding, and this leads to mistrust. Mistrust leads to further strain in the relationships between people who then prefer to hide themselves behind the veil of untruth or prejudice. Pent up feelings lead to anger, and anger to either depression or violence.

Everything starts in the minds and the hearts of people. Thoughts and feelings are the drivers of a person's life, leading him to destinations that he himself has charted out either consciously or in the dark corners of his subconscious mind. When both these drivers, the thoughts and the feelings, are encouraged to open up and express themselves without fear and thus be either influenced by, or influence the views of those around, the atmosphere changes, and people start understanding one another. Mahatma Gandhi preached that all beings have the innate capacity to love and understand, and it is to such capacity that we need to appeal to and direct our actions.

The problem is how to encourage people to open up and share their ideas and feelings. This requires some training, most easily accomplished when the process of education starts during the mother's pregnancy, during pre-natal care and preparation for motherhood. It then follows at an early stage of the child's development, where the near and dear ones, parents and teachers, become guides and friends, instilling trust, love, empathy and fearlessness amidst the children. The fear of being remonstrated and punished compels people to shield themselves, close all doors to outsiders who may hurt them. This is where the pursuit of the Sukhi Parivaar program, starting in the home early and followed up on a daily basis, can be a very effective way to instill trust, love, empathy and fearlessness amidst the people.

The earlier we include the program in our families, especially when the children are small and malleable, the greater is the possibility of imprinting the positive attitudes and values that enrich our lives. However it is never too latc to start. With adolescents and adults it takes more time, more convincing, more appeal to reason, and trust develops only when we ourselves become living examples to those observing us around. Where there is a will, there is a way.

When we start having a gradual awareness of the self, starting in the womb, life becomes a journey where along with genetic influences that express themselves only when fertile environment is present, it is our thoughts and actions that shape the future. And appropriate education helps us to move in the right direction. We cannot let ourselves drift in this sea of life without taking the oars in our hands, taking the boat in the direction we wish. We cannot rely on fortune alone. Some people rely on letting things happen. Why bother when the Lord who has brought us to life is there to take care of us? Like the birds and the beasts that roam in nature! True, He is there to take us along, but as humans endowed with the capacity of reasoning, this happens mostly on the path that we have ourselves embraced.

We reap what we sow! And if we sow the right seeds as per the dictates of the physical and spiritual Laws of Nature, the harvest will be positive. Sometimes we desire results fast, but forget the edict that we have the right to our actions, but not to the fruits thereof, fruits that will truly come when the time is ripe. Just look at our own lives and see who decided when the results of our actions would materialize. Remember the proverb: 'Man proposes and God disposes!'

The Sukhi Parivaar program is based on an understanding of the physical and spiritual Laws of Nature to the extent that our limited minds could comprehend. Our old scriptures have been the inspiration, and modern scientific findings based on social, medical, psychological and pedagogic studies have been the recipe. Research findings on fetus studies before birth, child rearing and pedagogy, and human behavior have helped trace the chart that is being proposed. Much work is still ongoing to explain why humans react in one way or another, but old and recent findings have given the indication for our future course. We hope parents, teachers, social workers, researchers and policy makers will find this book interesting and useful.

With immense possibilities of gene therapy that allows early detection of inborn abnormalities and offers ways and means to remedy them, with new findings of pedagogical and social research, we can safely say that the future is in our own hands! The Sukhi Parivaar program, with its stress on family communion and dialogue, is the start, and thereon can enable us to bring these possibilities to our doors. Only effort and optimism lead to progress. It is not utopic, but a conscious effort by everyone of us to assume our responsibilities as a member of the wider global community, the global family.

> *'Whatever you can do, or dream you can, begin it.*
> *Boldness has genius, power and magic in it.'*
>
> ***—Goethe***

Chapter II

An Overview

'Learning to be aware of feelings, how they arise and how to use them creatively so they guide us to happiness, is an essential lifetime skill.'

—Joan Borysenko

Understanding and applying the Power of Family Communion can lead to the concept of 'Sukhi Parivaar' or the 'Happy Family'. As the name suggests, it is a program that aims to bring happiness and peace in family life, and hence the society in general. Today, there is the general belief that our society is seriously sick. The society being made up of families, if only the individual families are taken care of, the society will be a different one, a better and happier one.

Our lives start in our home, amidst our kiths and kins, and it is in this home that the seeds of peace and happiness are first sown. After the seeds are sown, if the nurturing is faulty, unhappiness caused by mistrust, violence, injustice, greed, oppression, insecurity, alcoholism, drug addiction, disease, divorce, suicide, etc. take root. The home is the real nursery for bringing a happy society. Then only schools, socio-cultural organizations, religious bodies and the Government can have a supplementary and complementary positive role.

Where Wealth Accumulates and Men Decay

We may have tons of money, big house with all amenities, bungalow and yacht by the sea-side, limousines and everything that brings material comfort, but if there is no peace and harmony in the home, life is like in a hell! On the other hand, we may be materially poor, earning just enough to live from hand to mouth, but if our wife and children are loving and caring and there is complete harmony and understanding between all the members, happiness is visible on their faces. Modern couples think that money can bring happiness in their lives. Both partners work to earn more so as to afford the extra home gadget and luxury, and spend on their children. Little do they realize that spending more time with their children is more beneficial than the extra material benefits they acquire and the money they can earn!

A study conducted at the University of Chicago by Susan E Mayer[1] brings out that doubling the income of the poorest Americans had disappointing results. It would barely reduce dropout rates of children, and had very small effect in reducing teenage pregnancy. It would barely improve child outcomes overall. Money alone is not the criterion!

True, happiness is a state of the mind, but this state is only possible if we are at peace within ourselves and we share our joys and sorrows as one family unit, and help one another. Such peace and happiness then radiate from us and touch all members of the society, ending in global peace and happiness.

'Ill fares the land where wealth accumulates and men decay', so said the poet Oliver Goldsmith years ago. Today we see this trend in so-called developed societies where there is every material comfort, but where there is greed, disharmony, constant violence both within and outside the home. Families are being dismantled with single parent homes, divorce rates increasing, young adolescents on sex rampage, adults and some parents becoming pedophiles and even taking to incest, many adults not willing to take the risk of marriage and have children. One wonders what has happened to basic ethics and morality! Many believe they have only one life to live, and it is **their** life. Their needs come first. Why should they bother about others? This disease is spreading like wild fire with the impact of modern communication, and if responsible people do not face it and make necessary changes to their living and thinking, the future of humanity is at risk. Many countries and societies already crave for a morsel of such happiness often lost in fairy tales!

The Main Foundation and Objective

It is in the minds of people that violence and wars are born. As per this UNESCO edict, it is in the minds of men that the seeds of peace and harmony have to be sown.

Education, supported by mutual love, understanding and empathy, sharing of common bonds, adequate communication among members, becomes the main foundation for any society that aims at evolving into a model nation, and a torchbearer of peace and harmony in the world.

The program of 'Sukhi Parivaar' or Happy Family aims at awakening all of us to our duties and responsibilities, starting in our own family units. It thus enables us to take necessary actions pro-actively. We are responsible for what we see around us, and if we play our roles properly, we can stem the tide of violence and make our home, our community, our country and the world a better place. We have to assume our primary responsibility.

Hence, the campaign has an **objective** to transform the society so that we can eliminate the evils that plague us in our world. Transformation has to start in the primary unit that is the family. And this involves the participation of all members of the family, from the oldest grandparents to the youngest children. Everyone is a stakeholder, as the happiness of every member is intricately linked with the happiness of the other, and eventually that of the society.

Passing the Buck

In modern times we tend to delegate and often relegate this task to schools, (pre-primary, primary, secondary and tertiary), and to socio-cultural, socio-religious, and socio-economic organizations, and when things fail, we blame the Government or the politicians of the day! Our schools and colleges have their own program, mostly centered on career orientation, with little value-based education. Our socio-religious leaders are often concerned with increasing their followings and building 'empires' of their own. Our governments are busy promoting economic growth and ensuring higher living standards. And our politicians, busy in ensuring their following. What are our family members doing? What we ignore is the fact that it is the family that has to play the crucial role; for it is there that everything takes root, and is nurtured.

With the advent of radio and television, computers and multimedia gadgets, coupled with an often misguided formal educational system, the pressure of time is creating undue havocs on our mutual relationships at home. We have little time for the others. The family as a cohesive unit is being dismantled. People are becoming more self-centered, thinking that they have one life and it is theirs to live fully. Marriages are not lasting. Young adults are no more interested in marriages and having children, who are looked at as liabilities! And we take it as a matter of fact. What we forget is that it is up to us to shape our destiny, and take the necessary steps that can transform our lives. We are responsible for our own happiness or destruction! Blaming others for what we experience is just escapism. Modern civilization is our own creation!

The Central Idea

The central idea about 'Sukhi Parivaar' or Happy Family is that we must devote at least half an hour daily, in the early morning or evening, sitting together and communicating with one another in the family. This is like a time for **communion** with the family spirit. **It includes a few minutes of common prayer, followed by sharing one another's achievements and problems, joys and sorrows.** This is the only way to strengthen bonds, and impart family values within. Communication, frank communication, polite communication is all that is missing! Devoting half an hour daily is not much to ask from responsible people, concerned with the welfare of the family members.

The daily exercise consists of the following aspects:

Parenting in Practice

1. Resolve and meet daily for HALF HOUR, before or during meals.
2. Turn off TV, radio, mobile phone.
3. Say a prayer in a language all understand.
4. Father relates his day's experience.
5. Mother relates her day's experience.

6. Each child relates his/her day's experience.
7. Polite exchange of views on current topics.
8. Continue conversation at dinner table.
9. Involve children in buying groceries, planning meals and once weekly in cooking together.
10. Speak openly on social evils and on our responsibility.

Transferring Values

Where grandparents are alive and share the common roof, they can learn about the problems of their children, and offer whatever advice they can. They can tell stories of the lives of heroes from the epics to the grandchildren, and inculcate eternal values at an early age. They can transfer such values with love and understanding, so that when children grow up, they already have the seeds of these values to germinate and shape their lives. Absence of values, ethical, moral, and spiritual, in our educational system is the main cause of conflict and violence in society.

In nuclear families, parents, through such half hour sessions, can know more about their children's lives at school, and cultivate mutual love, trust and friendship with the kids. They can take appropriate decisions on how to help the children in their homework and provide them with proper guidance. In the absence of grandparents, they can themselves inculcate values that will mark the lives of the children. As children grow into adolescence, trust and love imbibed at home are critical for their future development.

A Daily Event

Such daily communion demands self-discipline on the part of all. Parents cannot advise their children not to smoke or take alcohol when they are themselves victim of these weaknesses. They cannot cheat or lie to the children for they will soon be caught. They cannot shout and ill-behave, as that will badly affect the young ones. They cannot fight between themselves, as husband and wife for that will be setting the wrong example. Their lives will be like an open book that their children will read and digest. Hence the concept of 'Sukhi Parivaar' demands self-reform for it to succeed.

Some people claim that they do often communicate at dinner table! This is not the type of communication we need. At dinner we have to concentrate on the food, relish it so that digestion is expedited, and exchange some pleasant small talks. On the other hand, during the half hour communion we aim at in the Sukhi Parivaar concept, this half hour before dinner is a sacred time when we really hope to open our hearts and share our joys and sorrows of the day, with the hope that such communication will bind us all the more.

The Program

The program starts with public gatherings during which organizers awaken the interests of parents, social leaders, teachers and religious preachers, and make them aware of the campaign, sometimes in the presence of important personalities. It is directed by knowledgeable social workers, and followed by a series of seminars and workshops in different parts of the country, involving the stakeholders, like in schools, community centers, parent teacher associations, socio-religious and socio-cultural organizations. In the seminars and workshops different tools like group therapy, family counseling, audiovisuals, role-model presentations, pamphlets, dramas, etc. are used for changing the way we think and act. Changing mindsets is not easy but not impossible! One has to be convinced of the idea and follow it up against all odds.

Today we see deterioration of family values, followed by the series of crimes, family violence, suicides, alcoholism, drug abuse and what not in the society. Tomorrow it will knock at our own doors, unless it has already done so, and we have to act now. The more we delay, the more the cancer will devour our lives. It is the sacred duty of each of us to take up the challenge and launch the 'Sukhi Parivaar' Happy Family campaign in our own circles.

At the global level, greed and excessive consumerism are leading to social and ethnic inequities, and the craving for power and pelf is corrupting minds. These in turn are leading to local and regional conflicts that often use religion as an anchor and banner. True religion is one in which the spirit of love and sharing is the guiding principle. And this principle is inherent in the concept of the Sukhi Parivaar and its strategy for family and social reform. Once every family reaches a state of peace and harmony in the spirit of sharing, supporting and loving one another, the society will be different. Only dialogue and open heart to heart communication will open the lock to this ideal. The work starts in the home of each and every one of us!

The power of family communion is limitless, and forms the bedrock of civilized living.

HUMANITY

'You must not lose faith in humanity. Humanity is like an ocean;

if a few drops of the ocean are dirty, the ocean does not become dirty.'

—*Mahatma Gandhi*

Chapter III

The Story of the Little Sparrow

'We ourselves feel that what we are doing is just a drop in the ocean. But the ocean would be less because of that missing drop.'

—Mother Teresa

Once a forest was ablaze with fire[2] that was destroying every nook and corner, and spreading wild. The King of the forest was helpless, and all his Ministers and Advisors were unable to offer any viable suggestion or take any appropriate action. They just kept consoling themselves with the feeling that the end of the world had finally stuck. Nobody could oppose the dictates of destiny! God had ordained that it be so.

The Ministers and the Advisors kept saying 'It's not me. It's him the possible culprit!' They were pointing fingers at one another, accusing one another for either not having foreseen the event, or for having done the wrong thing earlier, and triggered the calamity. And the fire was now reaching their doors! The King's Cabinet met in emergency and after a prolonged and heated deliberation eventually decided that everyone should evacuate the area. Even before that decision, many had already fled from their homes and taken refuge in another country where they felt themselves and their family secure!

The flocks of docile deer, the antelopes, the lions and tigers, the hogs and mongooses, the serpents and reptiles, the big and small birds, in fact every mobile inhabitant of the forest was running for life. Why has God been so cruel as to inflict such an undeserving fate to us, so they thought! And the fire was behind them. If they stopped to breathe, they ran the risk of being consumed! The sky was red far away, and dark with smoke overhead. Breathing was a problem. Some were carrying their old folks on their back, while others, too weak to run, accepted their fate and got consumed.

The atmosphere was rent with the wails of the dying, the thundering clapping of the fire, and the parents calling for their near and dear ones. The end of the world, oft described in the ancestral scriptures, had come!

While everyone was running for life, in the midst of this pandemonium, was a lone little sparrow that did not do like the others. It flew quickly to the river nearby, came back with a few drops of water in its beak, and dropped them in the blazing fire. It then went back as fast as possible to the river and returned with the few water drops that it threw on the fire. Again it rushed to the river and repeated this exercise ceaselessly.

The King noted this activity, and called the sparrow:

- Hey little bird! What are you doing, risking your life? Are you such a fool as not to realize that your few drops will never quench the fire?
- Sir, I am not foolish! I am doing my duty. Just imagine if every creature in this forest did what I am doing, everyone playing one's rightful role during this crisis, would we not be able to quench the fire?

The King was dumbfounded! He realized the wisdom of the little sparrow's act.

The Moral of the Story

If only everybody realizes his or her duty, either as a member of a family or as a concerned citizen, any crisis can bc tackled and calamity avoided. The realization of one's duty is the first step towards security, progress and happiness. Proper education should awaken this realization early in life.

How can this realization be achieved? Where do we start? There are so many priorities in life, and the first is self-preservation, which, as we say, is the first law of nature. But few realize that in this complicated world, self-preservation can only be effective in a gregarious society when the actions are such as to simultaneously affect the lives of those around. If we live in a society, we have to share responsibilities and be a team player. Proper education at school and in the home should emphasize the role of cooperation, of working together as a team.

However much we extol individual distinction, such distinction has no meaning if it contributes nothing to the welfare and progress of living beings. It is the excessive spirit of such distinction that leads towards cutthroat competition, towards exploitation of the weaker sections of society and to gross injustice. It is such wrong orientation that leads to pronounced individualism, and the oft heard statement from our children of: 'This is my life!' Such individualism leads to egoism and little regard for others, with little or practically no spirit of sharing.

Some philosophies emphasize individual salvation, forgetting that this is not possible as long as we are members of a society. Such salvation can only be a form of temporary illusion!

Today, like the forest, our society and our globe are on fire, and we are paying the price of such development with global warming and a series of catastrophes and crisis. Be it in the realm of physical environment or in the realm of economic welfare, the world is suffering. There is now a longing for another world where the spirit of love, fellow-feeling, sharing and mutual trust can prevail. We can create this new world. It is all in our hands. We are responsible for what we make of our lives. This is where there is a need to develop a Happy Family or the Sukhi Parivaar, starting from the very basics of development.

If everybody could act like the little sparrow, contributing one's mite with devotion and self-sacrifice, we would have another world!

CHAPTER IV

Spirit of Competition or Spirit of Sharing?

Competition strengthens the strong, while sharing empowers the weak, and fosters mutual love.

—Anon

Everyone is responsible for all.
Everyone alone is responsible.
Everyone alone is responsible for all.

—Antoine de Saint-Exupery

This is a politically charged question! The race for material fulfillment has led to a spirit of cutthroat competition and growing mistrust. Mistrust in the family, mistrust in the work environment, mistrust in society and mistrust at global forums dominate our life around. Individualism is the norm, and people are encouraged, through the current education, to compete rather than to share. The result is that we have forgotten the essential oneness of mankind and are running after the neck of one another in this inhuman race. The direct effects are global warming, climate change and related environmental problems as well as the global financial crisis that are arousing us to opt for another way of living.

Drastic cultural changes are fast transforming our society. There was a time when socialization was prevalent, with individuals meeting and sharing views and ideas, and bonding with one another. Today this is rare, and we are either in front of the TV or the computer, lost in a world where our contact, physical, emotional and spiritual, with our family members and with members of the society, is minimal. People used to meet at the dinner table, on the roadside, at the corner shop, at the club or in the park bench and share experiences with family members, neighbours and those in the community. Today, in many places, we hardly know them, and if we do to some extent, it's through Facebooks, Twitter and other computer programs that keep us physically away from one another. You cannot read the body language properly, nor understand the other person properly, and individualism as a culture spreads like wild fire. With individualism we have the consequent mistrust.

Many people cite the great 'progress' made in the little state of Singapore as an example of development to emulate. Yes, there has been great material and economic development, with clean areas, sky-scrapers, a multitude of fast motorways, and efficient and competitive work-force. But do we realize that beneath this veneer there is growing emotional insecurity, blood pressure rising, a sense of hurry as if all life is a race to amass more wealth. The youth have little or no family life. They refuse to get emotionally tied to the opposite sex, and to get married and have children. So much so that the Government has to rely more and more on imported labor amidst an ever-aging population. In Singapore they are even sponsoring holiday camps where young men and women can meet, share some moments together, and possibly get bonded with the desire to marry and settle down and have children. I wonder how much the government is spending on such programs![3]

This does not imply that there has been no progress in human endeavors. Indeed, through the advancement of science and technology and the spread of democracy, people in many countries are better off and are capable of meeting most of their basic needs in terms of food, shelter and clothing. Life-spans have increased globally thanks to health care systems. Government have become more conscious of the need to combat the scourge of disease and want, and the need to empower the people. In most countries, with some exception, slavery[4] and oppression of the weaker sections of the society have disappeared, as was the norm a few centuries ago. But feudal systems have not totally disappeared, nor have poverty and want. The grueling poverty in Sudan, as depicted in the web link in the footnote, is an eye-opener. Many global problems are being tackled by the organizations of the United Nations system, but we still have to struggle to imbibe a global spirit of solidarity and mutual love and compassion.

A Common Destiny

Slowly we are realizing that we share a common destiny on this blue-green planet. As humans we share over ninety-nine percent of our genetic makeup, and have to live in harmony with one another and with nature, taking out of this nature only that bare minimum we need, and giving back to it where possible what we temporarily destroy. For the resources are limited and we have to preserve for future generations if we do not want to become extinct as a species. Our blue-green planet is slowly dying with increasing fever, and its natural resources are being depleted so fast that, it is claimed, we would need four more similar planets to enable us survive with this pattern of consumption. Biodiversity has suffered a terrible shock and partial demise within the last few generations, and in some areas, the chirping of a bird, the flutter of a butterfly, the croaking of a toad, and even the babble of a small child is disappearing!

The **culture of mistrust** that individualism and competition have strengthened is making it extremely difficult for people of goodwill to create bridges of mutual trust. Because of mistrust the elimination of poverty, disease, hunger, exploitation and wars and weapons of mass destruction is a constant problem. The ratification of international treaties on environment, nuclear wars and nuclear terrorism by powerful nations is still an issue at international forums. The Comprehensive Nuclear Test Ban Treaty is a case in point where mistrust among nations is fast leading to the proliferation of deadly nuclear weapons in many 'rogue' states. Our blue-green planet and its inhabitants are under constant threat.

Religiosity versus Spiritualism

As a revolt against different forms of exploitation, religious fundamentalism is on the rise in spite of higher literacy levels. We are also slowly realizing that our religious differences are our own creation, and that spiritualism rather than religiosity has to be the way ahead.

Spiritually we are all united as children of one human family, of the same Creator, and only this realization can bring happiness through love, peace and harmony. Besides universal values of love, peace, and harmony, we have to imbibe the spirit of truth, compassion, social justice, sharing and non-violence. Then only we can replace mistrust, prejudice, hatred and disunity by the spirit of sharing and understanding. Many of our power-hungry leaders who thrive on the policy of divide and rule are misled, and it is our bounden and sacred duty to bring them within the spiritual fold of humanism. This is easier said than done! But humanity's struggle towards the elimination of greed and hatred, of eliminating domination by empowerment of the weak, and by spiritual regeneration of all, has to continue until love becomes all pervasive. While hatred divides, love unites. While division weakens, unity strengthens.

This is where the spirit of competition has to yield to the spirit of sharing and uniting through love and compassion. The global agenda of the dominant class promoting competition when the starting point is different and the grounds uneven, where level playing fields are absent, is questionable. When one partner is weaker, competition will only be destructive. Sharing and empowerment should then prevail. In any society, as in a family, we have the weaker members and the stronger members. The stronger members' duty is then not to promote competition but sharing and empowerment. Then only we can achieve a happier family, a united family. The same is the case of the nation and the globe where all are members of the human family.

Today even brothers and sisters in the same home, aspiring to outshine through competition, are not willing to help one another! In some universities where the highest standards of conduct and education are expected, academic colleagues are unwilling to share notes so that they have an edge in the academic promotion exercise. Teamwork involving people from various disciplines is a problem, with the result that their research output is meager in terms of impact, as it has not contributed to social and economic development in their midst. Individual excellence with publications in international research journals has not often promoted global impact and humane development.

Does all this mean that there should be no competition? Not at all! **Competition should be encouraged, but it should be competition with oneself. Everybody, including the child, should be given the tool to evaluate himself/herself, and enabled to achieve a goal.** Even the area of sports, sadly, is suffering from the disease of corruption where individuals and teams are bent on minting money. Excellent sportsmen are on sale at a global level! Is it not so in football and cricket teams? The individual should ensure that his/her activities are helping to improve himself/herself and the surroundings. When the person looks at the mirror in the morning, the question that is to be asked is: 'Am I better than what I was yesterday? Have I contributed to making the world any better? Have I spread trust and the spirit of sharing around?'

Competition in Everyday Life

In the education system, continuous assessment should replace end-of-year examinations. At home, a continuous monitoring of the younger ones by the elders, and self-appraisal of the elders must be ensured through the Sukhi Parivaar program. In work environments and in industries, continuous innovation and improvement of services and products must be encouraged. Increased profit in companies should not be an end in itself. Profits must be shared to ensure that the workers and the community are benefiting from such achievements. Workers must be made shareholders of the companies.

Instead of encouraging cutthroat competition for enhanced economic growth, maximization of profits and increasing disparities between the top management and the rest, there should be a limit to what people can earn to ensure that they have a better quality of life. We are interdependent as a global community, and just as in a family, the strong should assist the weak to come up. Empowerment of the masses through sharing rather than strengthening the power of the strong through competition should be the norm.

Otherwise, the strong will spend billions and trillions of dollars just to safeguard its edge by unethical means like stockpiling of weapons of mass destruction, and encouraging uneven competition and unfair global trade. Manufacture and trade in arms, unending wars and border disputes, the race to wield global power and 'colonize' the less developed countries, grabbing of natural resources and self-enrichment are all related to the spirit of competition where greed stays as the basic element.

Such a spirit of competition will only perpetuate conflicts at all levels, within families and nations. Admittedly the world is not all made of good people, but should this prevent us from forging a better one?

Chapter V

Where is Modern Development Taking Us?

'Only when the last tree is cut, only when the last river is polluted, only when the last fish is caught, only then will we realize that we cannot eat money.'

—Cree Indian Proverb

All human beings want to be happy in the midst of relatives and friends, living in a healthy environment where the bounties of Nature are accessible to all, and where there is peace, harmony and human development. Human development has two main components: the material and the spiritual, and it's only when the two are balanced so that we are in harmony with the forces of Nature that true development can take place. It is said that modern development has stressed too much on the material aspect, with less and less importance to the spiritual aspect of life. This is being confirmed by the excesses of industrial development, unbridled energy consumption, greed with no limit to accumulation of profits, thus leading to global warming and climate change. The sad consequences of such development are only now being gauged by development pundits.

On the material side our priority is to meet the basic needs like food, shelter and clothing, along with physical health, employment and education. On the spiritual side we need the development of an aesthetic sense, a spirit of love, sharing, compassion, and the realization of our self, with the understanding of our place in the grand order of things. It is a pity that modern education does not cater for all these. There is too much stress on academic and professional achievements with the objective of the individual securing a well-paying job that can enable him or her to afford the luxuries of modern living.

Post Industrial Revolution

Families had different roles and status in the pre-industrial period. The members were well knit and depended on one another. They were responsible for ensuring adequate hands for food production, and for socialization and education. When industrialization started, new work and living conditions forced members to depend on others for food production, education and social support during times of illness and old age. Government had to assume greater responsibility for the care of the citizens, along with so many other environmental problems. From self-sufficiency we moved to greater and greater dependence on others outside the family, and thus to more and more individualism. Family ties diminished.

'With the advent of the Industrial Revolution two and a half centuries ago, a new culture of consumerism has developed, with ruthless exploitation of the limited resources of the world. Respect for nature has diminished, with the belief that all that exists on this globe is for human consumption! **Existentialism** as a philosophy has become rampant in the developed world. People believe in one life that has to be lived to the full, irrespective of what happens to others and other forms of life. There is little if any, respect for other forms of life on the planet.'[5] Our economists have to share much of the burden for this!

BOX 1: A British Picture

David Willetts, a senior-British politician, foresees that with the increasing number of family break-ups, marriages could become an affluent elite middle-class institution. Following the American trend, people on low or insecure jobs do not get married. Marriage rate in Britain, 2009, is at half the rate in 1972. The less educated women born after 1960 have divorce rate 30% higher than the better educated, and are less likely to have a child outside a live-in partnership.

"I think there are things that have gone deeply wrong with our country. The rate of family break-ups is a disaster for children." He advocates for a better recognition of marriage in the tax system, and steps to bolster marriage. The state and the voluntary sector should help fathers in their relationship, especially at the birth of the first child when many couples break up.

Indo-Asian News service, Dec. 2009.

After the industrial revolution with its stress on production based on economies of scale and profit maximization, a new breed of economists spurred by humanism came up. John Galbraith in the 1950's and Ernst Frederic Schumacher[6] in the 1970's were both influenced by Gandhian concept of new patterns of decentralized production with possibilities of increased job creation and minimal energy consumption.

Physical and Social Environment

We have seen that our natural physical environment is being polluted by the typc of dcvelopment the world is emulating, and leading to health problems with new diseases and new viruses. What are the consequences on the social environment?

On the social environment, the development of self-centered individualism is slowly leading to the disappearance of some. In developed countries the population growth rate is generally negative, while in developing countries emulating the developed world, population growth rates are either stagnating or becoming negative, with some exceptions. People are encouraged to have fewer children in order to cope with poverty and growing food demands. The few who are born are encouraged or taught to imitate the life styles of the developed world.

In the developed world where people enjoy often very high standards of living, the young adults are unwilling to have children and set up a proper family. To most of them having children is a liability that they do not want to have. They prefer to spend whatever they earn on themselves, affording whatever luxury they feel like enjoying.

Marriages are becoming rarer, and the trend is towards 'living together', where they do not have proper contract of allegiance. They change partners many times within their life. Children born out of wedlock are catered for by the government. Needless to say, such children grow up in an atmosphere of insecurity and lack of family love. Their emotional development is thereby distorted, and invariably crime rates are increasing.

From good old joint families we moved to nuclear families, and now to one-parent family or no family! Individualism has its heyday!

The virtues of living in a joint family system are extolled by the old ones that still remember their childhood days with nostalgia. They were poor, often living from hand to mouth, but were sharing the fruits of their labor with the rest of the family, participating in the common joys and sorrows. They had family support when needed, and their emotional development was secured. Family values were transferred from one generation to another through such sharing and participation, and crime rates were low. Alas, such days are fast disappearing.

We boast about countries like China and India doing extremely well in their economic development, but ignore the social repercussions of such fast economic growth. The pressures of trying to live a decent life have their toll of the mental and physical health of the people. In China the situation is becoming alarming with the butchery of innocent children in schools, even in kindergartens, by people, including teachers, who find no other ways to vent their resentment against the society and the system.

The box below gives a vivid account of what is happening in a society trying to mimic development patterns based on pure economic growth with trickle down effects.

BOX 2: Avenging against the Society

A series of five attacks within two months has marked the society in China. The last one was in a village in Shanghai in the North, where a 48 years old man, armed with a big Chinese kitchen knife, attacked a kindergarten and hacked to death seven children and their teacher. This followed four other attacks in other places, and in most cases the criminals committed suicide after the massacres. One was a 42 years old medical doctor who was having affective and professional problems. All the others were frustrated in a similar way.

Ma Ai, a psychologist from the University of Law and Political Science in Peking, commenting on these crimes, said: 'We have concentrated on economic development, but have neglected the development and improvement of the psychical side of the being. These recent events are a warning. Society is an ecosystem based not only on nature and the economy but also on the mental health of the population. Without this equilibrium the foundations are not healthy. We need a much better social ecosystem in future.'

Crime has increased significantly in China where 173 million adults suffer from mental problems.

Growing Old

Old people now end up in homes where the state, the church, or socio-cultural organizations contribute to their sustenance. Many feel extremely lonely for lack of their children's love. Very often we see them alone sitting in a garden, brooding, and if ever we make an effort to approach them and start a small conversation, they feel so happy to have somebody with whom to share their moments. Mental depression, Alzheimer's disease, and senility are common amongst them even if they are in the homes for the elderly. In most countries of the world it is recognized that within this century the number of old people will far outnumber the young ones, and expenses on their upkeep will be the dominant government concern. Medical expenses, as we all know, become more burdensome during old age. The pension schemes, wherever they exist, are wary about such eventualities. In such circumstances, nobody wants to become old, and suicide and death are the only liberation.

The following old-Chinaman's story in Box 3 is an another eye-opener!

BOX 3: The Old Chinaman's Story

Once, in a remote village in China, lived an old Chinaman and his small family. He lived with his son who was already in his fifties, his grandson who was in his early twenties, and his daughter in law. His own wife had passed away long long back, and he relied on his son to take care of him.

He was so old that the weight of the years had bent his back, and his body was all wrinkled and weak. He could hardly walk even with a stick, and had to be carried around on the back. In such condition he could naturally not work and be of any use to his family. As such, his son felt, he was a useless burden, and had to be disposed of.

As was the practice in that community, such old people were taken on the top of a mountain where he was left to die in a cave or be devoured by wild animals. That was the fate waiting for this old man!

One morning his son decided to take him on this last trip. He consulted his own son who, as an enterprising youth, advised that they construct a small cart as the road was long and difficult.

Together, the father and the son made this cart with the strong wood available. They placed the old man in the cart and started the journey. The old man looked very sad, as he knew that he would be left on the mountain to die alone, as was the fate of such people.

After the son, grandson and the old grandfather reached the top and located a suitable cave where to leave the old man, they very politely took the old man down, paid him their last respects, and bade him good bye. With tears in his eyes, the old man wished them well and turned his face.

Just when the father and the son were to start their journey down, the son decided to take the cart back rather than leave it there. The father remarked that it had served its purpose and was now of no use. But the young son remarked: 'Dad, I must carry this cart back, for I will need it when your turn will come to be left to die, just as grandfather!'

Then the man realized his folly! He realized how cruel he was towards his own father, and decided to take him back home and care for him to the end of his days. He took the old man on his back and carried him home.

Moral: Are we not committing the same crime when we take our old parents to homes and leave them there to die? When shall we wake up?

The Good Old Rural Life

Food production in itself has shifted from the multitude of small farmers to the few big multinational corporations using unsustainable means of production. Urbanization is increasing because of the wrong educational curricula promoting a spirit of white collared jobs and a dislike for menial agricultural jobs. The days of the common kitchen garden or the rural self-sufficient farmer are numbered! All in the name of modern development!

There was a time when rural life was the envy of educated people who extolled them in their literature. It was a life where simple living and high thinking was the norm. Villages were fairly self-sufficient. People grew enough food to nourish themselves, and a series of small and medium enterprises kept the economy alive. The land was always there to occupy the people. Now, with modern education, our children have taken a dislike for tilling the soil and producing our own food. How many trees have the modern generation planted in their back-yards? On the contrary they have felled down what their forefathers had planted.

Now, with rapid industrial development and consequent urbanization, life is becoming more hectic, stressful and the number of depressed people is fast increasing, along with crime rates.

Stress and Increasing Suicide Rates

A life of stress with inadequate family support and the trend towards individualization have increased suicide rates globally. Even in an Island Paradise like Mauritius[7] the latest World Health Organization figures show that there is one suicide every three days, and that suicides have increased by 20% between 2005 and 2007. Suicides are particularly amongst young adults who cannot cope with the competition or have partner problems. Financial problems are also the cause, and people are tempted to gamble so as to get some money. Gambling is becoming a scourge!

In Japan, one of the most developed countries of the globe, suicide is a growing problem, even amongst teachers who are stressed by parents who are outrageously demanding. Since the number of single parents is high, and also since the number of babies born is very low, parents have tendency to spoil their children by yielding to their whims. The competitive environment does not allow them to devote adequate time to the school-going children, and they depend more and more on the teachers for anything from feeding, laundry, nail-clipping to transport. Parents have been nicknamed as 'monster parents' by the media.[8] The Tokyo city government has had to publish a special handbook for teachers in public schools. Education there is highly commercialized!

With the financial crisis affecting many countries, private manufacturing firms, mostly multinationals, are downsizing and laying off many workers. With the objective of staying competitive, and in most cases keeping their profit margins high, many are moving to places like Bangladesh where labor costs are cheap, or importing cheap labor from such countries. This is particularly serious in the textile industries where the 'starvation' salaries given to the workers are only able to keep them alive in their poor conditions.

There is the case of a worker who has been in the trade for over thirty years, and who goes to the factory one morning and is given an envelope and asked to go home and not return to work anymore! He is required to collect his pay and retrenchment money amounting to a pittance, calculated according to the labor laws of the country, and stay away. Nobody cares whether the person has any debts for the education of his children or for medical conditions! Nobody cares if the person is having a sick child waiting for an operation! The person feels so despondent that the same day he commits suicide!

All that matters is that the firm stays competitive and keeps increasing its profits that are then invested into other firms for enlarging the business empire. That is the spirit that is being promoted by the gurus of market competition!

May be we cannot go back in time! But we can, with conscious efforts and far-sighted policies and programs, slowly move towards the less stressful rural life, with small industries spread out, giving jobs to all, as prescribed by Mahatma Gandhi and Ernst Frederic Shumacher. Our development policies and strategies can enable better living conditions where the quality of life is far more important than the standard of living. This needs a real change in mindset!

The Failure of Copenhagen Summit

Where is modern development taking us? The failure of COP15,[9] the United Nations Copenhagen world conference of climate change in December 2009, is the result of such development. But for a few awakened countries, developed countries that are mainly responsible for causing global warming are half-hearted about changing their life-styles and contributing adequately to reduce greenhouse gasses. On the other hand, some developing countries that have aspirations to enjoy life-styles similar to those of the developed countries, are unwilling to adopt new technologies that can reduce greenhouse gasses unless they get the resources for doing so from the developed countries. Resources are blocked by issues of intellectual property and other selfish motives. And the result is that we now run the risk of seeing the lives and the food and water supplies of billions of people endangered. And most of these people are from developing countries!

Post Copenhagen Summit, the US is struggling to present a bill on climate change, hoping to limit US carbon emissions by 17 percent by 2020. Large scale polluters will bear the brunt, while others will benefit from an incentive scheme that plans to spend up to US 2 billion dollars every year! That's where the money goes for dirty development!

So is the recent global financial crisis threatening the employment scene and the livelihood of hundreds of millions of people all around the world, in spite of the billions doled out as **Stimulus Package** to the very industries that, because of greed and mismanagement, caused this crisis. Again, the weak and the poor are and will be the main victims. We still do not know how long this crisis will continue.

Living Beyond Means!

Our problems stem from the current economic policies that encourage consumption in order to sustain economic growth. Marketing agencies make their profit by the techniques that are often questionable, and the average consumer is tempted to borrow and buy to satisfy himself. In the process indebtedness increases until these debts can no more be sustained, leading to bankruptcy. The good old saying that you have to cut your coat according to your cloth, as taught by our elders, is sent to the dustbin!

Is it not an irony that the most civilized area of the globe, namely Europe, is the most indebted region these days? The most industrialized countries in the world, including Japan, are the most indebted countries! Professor Stephane Garelli[10] of the Institute for Management Development (IMD), based in Switzerland, has warned: *'Budget deficits today have reached summits, and it is estimated that the average debt in countries of G20 will climb from 76% of their GDP in 2007 to 106% in 2010.'* There is need to bring down this debt to 60% of the GDP, as proclaimed in the Euro zone at Maastricht. While it will take 75 years to do this in Japan, other countries in Europe will take around 25 years! This is how the consumerist development has mortgaged a whole generation! Would you believe that Japan (June 2010) has the largest debt in the industrialized world?

Those that have greater external debt have reached a stage where the economies are no more sustainable, as in Greece, Spain and Portugal. These countries are already in crisis as they are no more financially credit-worthy, and cannot get additional loans to survive.

When national governments, regional organizations and banks along with international funding institutions like the World Bank and the IMF have to shell out millions of dollars just to enable the people to stay employed and not exacerbate social instability in a context of global financial crisis, we can ask ourselves: where did we go wrong? The answer is blowing in the wind! Look within our own souls and we will realize.

The European Union[11] along with the International Monetary Fund have just pumped a trillion US dollars just to save Greece, Spain and Portugal, and to prevent other states from running bankrupt! They have set up a Special Purpose Vehicle, the European Financial Stabilization Mechanism to ensure stability in Europe. And this is happening in one of the most developed and civilized areas of the globe! Such amounts could have assisted millions of people in other less developed countries to meet their basic needs, to follow an environmentally sound development path, and to maintain peace and security globally. It's time to wake up!

At whose expense are all these 'stimulus packages' and bailing out met, we may ask! It is obvious that those developing countries that really need support from the 'developed' countries will be penalized for lack of aid or loans. And who will suffer most? It's the already poor who are unable even to meet their basic needs while others enjoy the best.

Thank God, common sense is dawning on those 'developed' countries that are now trying to reduce their expenditures and straiten their belts! Investors are also reacting, and in the US, the well known banking giant, Goldman Sachs[12] was sued and agreed to pay billions of dollars in order to settle civil fraud charges of misleading investors. Meanwhile, the top bosses of the banks have been giving themselves sky-rocketing salaries and fringe benefits that have not been questioned. Now President Obama is trying to remedy the situation by legislation to cap such salaries.

We mentioned earlier about the type of education and its tendency to develop an extreme sense of individualism. The spirit of sharing and solidarity is now the domain of non-governmental organizations that have the responsibility to undertake projects that can bring back a sense of belonging and mutual support. The spirit of aggressive competition promoted by such development pits one member of the family against another. In the same house, one brother who is at school, preparing for examinations, does not want to share notes with another for fear of losing the competitive edge. Often, in business circles, they are prepared to kill one another to safeguard their interests.

How Sukhi Parivaar is Essential

The above issues should be the concern of one and all. All this can be altered with the practice of the Sukhi Parivaar program that allows us to support one another, monitor the development of family members through daily family communion. Community health, extended employment prospects, reduced stress and suicide rates, thrift, impacts of global warming, and values that enrich life can be discussed in the home and solutions found. Positive family and ancestral values can then be inculcated by responsible parents who themselves have to change their way of living for the benefit of the children. Teachers at schools and colleges will better understand their roles and provide the proper education. And the trained graduates will have another view of development.

Let us see the type of elite that our system is producing. The second box relates a story told to me by a Ghanaian father who felt disappointed and helpless.

It is such elite that, with the desire to grow rich fast and have all possible luxuries, get easily tempted by systemic corruption. Accepting various gifts, giving undue favors, abusing of one's authority and privileges, paying oneself exorbitant salaries, ..., the series can continue, and our governments, decision makers and managers are helpless. Mind change has to start in the womb and the cradle, and continue all through life in view of changing circumstances.

And it has to start in the home!

BOX 4: The Ghanaian Professor

Professor Adusa had reached his retirement age in the Ghanaian Civil Service, and was to leave office in a few months. While we were having lunch together during an international conference, we started speaking about modern education and its pitfalls. He then related his own experience at home.

'My son got his education in one of the prime schools in town, and completed his studies as a Chartered Accountant. The first salary he got was double that I was getting after nearly forty years of dedicated service. We were all very happy and proud for his success!

After starting work he stayed with us, sharing the same house and kitchen, enjoying his mother's dishes. After a while I took the courage of talking to him about our family burdens. I had spent most of my earnings on his education, and now that I was retiring soon, I needed some support, especially as the cost of medicines were going up and up.

I told him: 'Son, now that you are earning well, could you contribute something towards the kitchen. I am not asking you to pay for your lodging, but at least you could give us some money for the kitchen.' Here is the reply:

> *Father, don't you realize that I have to save my money for buying a car, building a house and getting married? You don't need these but I do!*

The father was struck dumb. He had never realized that his own son would one day refuse to share in the family burden, and leave him to fend for himself. He then realized the folly of the modern education, with its promotion of individual development, with disregard for family development. At one time children were assets to the family, helping them in the daily chores, and being available when required. Now they are liabilities, and that is the reason few young people want to get married and have children of their own. Family values, sharing and solidarity are sheer jargons!

This is where modern development is taking us!

Chapter VI

Education Starts in the Womb

'If wrinkles must be written upon our brows, let them not be written upon the heart. The spirit should never grow old.'

—John Kenneth Galbraith

We generally believe that education starts after the birth of a child, and is imparted by the parents, the teachers, and the society where friends and leaders have a significant input. This, however, is not right. For even before the birth, education has started in the womb. The fetus is a living entity that has the capacity to react to positive or negative feelings.

The Development of a Person's Brain

The development of a person's brain and behavior has been the subject of countless scientific studies. [13] The one that deals with neural development in humans through studies involving Neuroscience and Developmental Biology won its author, Prof. Gerald Edelman, a Nobel Prize. He described how brain cells as well as complex nervous systems form during embryonic development and throughout life.

It is now accepted that a child's education starts when the baby is still in the womb, right from the very early stages of the embryonic development.[14] Even when the child is not yet born, it is subjected to external and internal impacts resulting from the mother's or the parent's moods and behavior. The fetus is affected thereby, and becomes aware of its environment soon after four months of development. That is why old scriptures prescribe that after baby's conception, the mother has to be protected in a secure environment, given all physical and psychological support, so that the baby in the womb has the best environment for growth.

Ceremonies in Some Cultures

In some cultures elaborate ceremonies are organized to celebrate and mark that stage of the unborn child's development! In one oriental culture, as soon as the woman realizes that her menstruation has stopped, and that physical signs reveal that she is pregnant, it is a great occasion to celebrate in the extended family. Special religious ceremonies are organized in the presence of close relatives, and sumptuous meals are shared. All these are done to give the pregnant mother a sense of importance and to mark the mutual support of the relatives. She is then confined to minimal household work and fed with appropriate diet, while being showered with gifts by the husband and in-laws. Even parents are given new clothes as gifts!

Pre-natal care enables the mother to be properly fed, loved by the husband and the rest of the family, and provided with appropriate mood enhancing distractions.

Husband-Wife Violence-Free Relationship

Few couples realize that a husband and wife dispute impacts negatively on the baby's development when the unborn is still in the womb! The verbal or physical blows received by the mother affect the brain and nerve development of the child. You can imagine what happens in the case of stressed mothers-to-be who are pregnant and the partners are not there to share the burdens! If they are there, polite exchanges between parents, the sounds of the environment, the mood of the mother, all have an impact on the child for **memory imprinting** has already started.

Scientific Findings on Brain Development

Scientific research using sensors, electro encephalography, magnetic resonance imaging and other techniques have shown that at sixteen weeks the unborn child tries to avoid glaring light. It starts responding to speech patterns when twenty weeks after conception. It starts responding to external music after twenty-five weeks, and after thirty weeks, it can sense the emotional problems the mother faces! That is why it is so important for parents to ensure a loving environment with peace and harmony in the house. They can be instrumental in shaping the child's feeling of security and happiness. The mother has the most critical role in guiding the unborn child's personality by ensuring positive thoughts and feelings in herself, for these will shape the growth and development of the unborn child, and affect the personality for the rest of its life. These facts are described in Dr. Verny's book quoted in the footnote above.

Again recent research has shown that one should not believe that our genes and their roles are unchangeable and cast in stone. David Shenk[15] in his book 'The Genius in All of Us' says that our genes interact with the surroundings, and are turned on or off all the time, thus enabling a person to do things by sheer dint of application, determination and repetition. Intelligence develops in response to environment and how we deal with it. Mediocrity is not built-in, and our abilities are not set in stone. As an example, taxi-drivers in London, with time, develop larger posterior hippocampus, as our brains adapt in response to the demands we put on them. These findings can give people hope to improve and develop.

These new findings should form part of pre-marital courses for couples, and be inculcated in pre-natal advice and care for would-be mothers. Only then the mothers can have better bonds with the babies developing in the womb even before their birth. The would be fathers should also be brought into the picture so that they cooperate with the partner.

Nature and Nurture

Today, when we see a child misbehaving from and early age, we attribute it either to wrong parenting after the child's birth or to genetic traits acquired from ancestors. Children born in violent families are bound to be inherently violent! So we wrongly believe! This is now questionable in view of research findings. True, certain physical characteristics are inherited, but most psycho-social characteristics are the results of the impacts of the environment during the development of the fetus before birth, and after, as per the parental care and support received, as well as those of the teachers and peers.

Pre-Marital and Post-Marital Counseling Essential

In the Sukhi Parivaar program, pre-marital advice is given to young people preparing to get married, on the need for developing appropriate mutual relationships. Newly married couples are advised to take the habit of daily communication between them so as to build the trust, love and harmony necessary in the budding family. When the wife is pregnant, the concepts highlighted in the above paragraphs are shared between the partners so that they understand the implications of their behavior and temperament on the fetus that is developing in the mother's womb. The physical development of the fetus is now known through biological findings, and has to be communicated to the couples. New studies on emotional development are in progress, and all show that the education of the child starts right in the womb.

Religious leaders are also educated as to their roles in promoting the above concepts.

We can now see why a person's development starts right from the time of his conception in the womb of the mother. It is therefore essential for appropriate action to start at this early stage if we want to ensure a proper growth and development of the person, and a happy family, where violence is reduced to the minimum, and where peace and harmony can prevail.

Chapter VII

The Ten Stages of a Person's Development

> *'It is through the idealism of youth that man catches sight of truth, and in that idealism he possesses a wealth which he must never exchange for anything else.'*
>
> ***—Albert Schweitzer***

Many theories on the stages of a human's development have been promulgated in the course of our history. The earliest goes back to the Vedic times when a person's life was divided into four stages: Period of education and celibacy, period of the householder with his family responsibilities, period of preparation for renunciation, and finally the period of renunciation when life is completely devoted to service of humanity. It is to be noted that life was not characterized by personal development alone, but had a pronounced social role. Later theories, because of the way post-industrial societies evolved, have stressed mostly on personal development stages. A very recent one is that of Erik Erikson[16] who has proposed eight stages. In this chapter we are proposing ten stages including the socio-cultural aspect where the last two stages define our social responsibility so as to ensure a happy society.

First Stage in the Womb

We have seen in the previous chapter how development starts in the womb of the mother. This is the **first stage,** a very critical stage that few people know about or understand, and that is generally ignored by the vast majority. If this stage is mishandled, physical and psychological complications that follow can wreck the life of the new born.

Security as Crux of Second Stage for Three Years

The **second stage** starts when the baby is born, and lasts for three years during which the mother's role as a care-taker is extremely important. The love and care of the mother and father cannot be replaced by the love and care of the nanny. Trained parents mould the mind of the child generally in a better way. This is the period when the child develops its oral senses. The mother's loving care along with her visual contact and touch **develops trust** in the baby, and this is essential for its outlook in later life. Trust being one of the major problems in modern society where a culture of mistrust is prevalent, has its beginnings during this early stage, up to three years of age. Erikson claims that **suicidal tendencies** in individuals develop when at this early stage the child feels insecure and believes that the world is not trust-worthy.

This is also the stage when the child learns to walk, talk, and feed itself, along with other skills. Developing self-esteem in the child, and not shaming him for acts not well done, are also critical. The parents' role in ensuring these is primordial. There is a tendency nowadays to send the child very early to a nursery because parents are not available to take care of the child. We can see how not taking personal care of the child during this period can have devastating effects. The mother should be there for the child at this stage, and developing nurseries to allow her to start work at this stage will only promote violence in the society. There is need to extend the period of maternity leave to enable the mother to take appropriate care of the baby in this initial stage of its development.

Pre-Primary School Stage

The **third stage** is when we send the child to **pre-primary school**, a tradition and a social necessity in the present times since our educational system is based on that. It would have been preferable if parents themselves could educate and take care of the child in this age group, but since the task is now in the hands of pre-primary teachers, we have to ensure that they are properly trained and are aware of the psychological needs of the child at this age. Normally this is the time when children learn to play with others and share toys. Their ego starts developing, and they like to imitate adults. The oedipal complex develops, and the care-takers have to see to it that they do not develop guilt complex through non-fulfillment of natural desires and through frustration.

Fourth Stage as Lower-Primary Schooling

The **fourth stage** is that between five and eight, the lower primary school age when children learn fast, and their memory power is very good. They are capable of memorizing full songs and texts that they start reading and writing. Language learning is fast, and in some cultures children of this age group can swim easily within five languages to which they are exposed. Basics of mathematics can be taught, and they are able to respond quite well. Once again parents and teachers have to be supportive and less critical, and instill self-confidence in the child.

The development of the child's brain is such that up to the age of eight, full attention has to be paid to the emotional and mental growth. In many old traditions the child joins school after the age of eight, for at this age the child's brain starts developing in a different way, and the memorizing power increases. Thus it is preferable for parents to pay more attention to the child, enable him or her to discover the environment around, and provide the full emotional support at home till that age.

Fifth Stage from Eight to Twelve

The **fifth stage is** from eight to twelve, during which the child starts developing greater reasoning. The child can learn different skills, and socialize easily, and if a sense of self-esteem is developed and encouraged by the elders, the child can do extremely well in life later. Generally between eight and twelve, the child is more obedient, and is influenced more by the teachers at school than parents at home. Teachers become role models. The child always feels that teachers know more than parents, and follow them, provided the psychological bonds are established.

Sixth Stage as Adolescence

The **sixth stage** is from twelve to eighteen when the child is normally in secondary school, and is an adolescent. During adolescence beyond the age of eleven or twelve, when hormonal changes become predominant, it becomes more difficult for parents to influence the child. Changes in the body development make him or her very self-conscious, and complexes are common. During this period the influence of the peers becomes more visible. The child has the tendency to question everything, and one has to be very cautious when advising him or her. Role models play much greater part in shaping their development. At school they learn some life skills along with academic subjects that prepare them for higher education.

Adolescence is the time when children seek their own identity while facing social interactions that mark them for good. They develop long lasting relationships. Their sense of morality is very high, and their idealism, when nourished, can make them develop into exceptional beings. Albert Schweitzer[17] said that if people can sustain the idealism of their adolescence, the world would be a much better place to live. 'Grow into your ideals, so that life can never rob you of them. If all of us could become what we were at fourteen, what a different place the world would be!' The youth should have ideals that are pure, strong and stable so that they eventually impact on overall development.

Seventh Stage at University

The **seventh stage** is between eighteen and twenty five when the person is normally, as in most countries, at the university, studying for a passport to a profession. Here the young adult learns to be more independent and fend for himself or herself. The individuality becomes more pronounced, while practical life experience is still wanting. The influence of parents is minimal. Parents should act more like friends and empathize with the children than act as authoritative parents. This is the time when girl friends or boyfriends have a special place in the lives of the young ones, and often end up as life partners through marriage. If such relationships before marriage fail, the young adults become frustrated and tend to trust less. In defense they develop a false sense of superiority and tend to become introverts. Finding other partner friends becomes an obsession and can affect the studies. If the relationships succeed in the early phases, they have the possibility of lifelong success in marriage.

Eighth Stage as Married Life

The next stage is the **eighth stage** of married life and family responsibility. This can last till sixty years of age or more. The Sukhi Parivaar concept, when sincerely practiced in this stage, can make a very happy family where love, peace, harmony and mutual trust and support become the norm. It is up to parents to initiate and sustain this family communion on a regular basis. The family has priority over other things, and job satisfaction becomes more likely when home relationships are congenial.

With the arrival of children, the parents feel bound to transfer values and culture to the kids, as responsible partners. They also find social responsibility as a necessity, as they feel that the society should reflect the values and norms they apply at home.

When children grow up and found their own independent families, parents then feel that their parental responsibility is over, and are likely to experience a void. They tend to fill it by commitment to the work place or the community. There they often feel that they lack something and need to re-educate themselves. Some resume studies to complete courses they had always wanted. Some take to meditation and yoga to search for meaning within themselves, which then leads us to the next stage in our development.

Stage after Retirement

The **ninth stage** usually starts after retirement from active service, and should be the stage of self-preparation for selfless service to the society. In some cultures they retire to a home for the retired where they follow specific courses. Or to secluded places where they practice active meditation and yoga, and study the scriptures to find meaning in life. After having acquired mastery over their senses and learnt new techniques to serve the society, they prepare to resume the life of ascetics in which the ego is reduced to minimum, and in which they consider themselves as a reflection of the self in other beings. Amongst the Hindus this is the 'Vanprastha stage'.[18]

Tenth Stage as Final Renunciation Stage

The **tenth stage,** or the last stage is that where the person has renounced all personal desires, and is only there to serve the society selflessly. The person has no family and considers the all humanity as his or her family. There is no fixed residence and the person keeps moving from one place to another, staying with whosoever offers hospitality, and serving the community through preaching righteous living to all, or through spreading the precepts of great people so as to transform the society. They possess no material wealth, and whatever is given to them as donation is used for philanthropic activities in social service. Such people are highly recognized for their dispassionate and selfless advice. Amongst the Hindus, this stage is called the 'Sanyasa' stage.

In this final stage the person is supposed to be fully developed, physically through practice of yoga, mentally through both formal and self-education, spiritually through meditation, and socially through active and selfless service to humanity at large. They tend to live for very long in such evolved state.

Holistic Development

These ten stages of human development offer a viable path for humanity if we aim at attaining sustainable development from all angles. If properly practiced, we can have a society almost free from the major evils that plague us. Happiness is not a vain word. The happy family is a real possibility, and worth living and working for.

We have been so much conditioned by the profit motivated broadcasts and the publications around, as well as by the lifestyles proposed to us by most of the rulers of the world, that we are rushing headlong into this mad race and forgetting that happiness starts with contentment and peace of mind, along with the feeling of personal advancement in harmony with Nature.

Chapter VIII

What's Happening to Our Kids in Schools?

> *'If we are to teach real peace in this world, and if we are to carry on a real war against war, we shall have to begin with the children.'*
>
> ***—Mahatma Gandhi***

Parents feel helpless, and teachers are blaming parents for what is happening in schools. The Government is keen to see improvements in discipline at schools and colleges, but the task is not that easy. Parent-teacher associations are just complaining, and asking for assistance from authorities to tackle the many problems. And the situation is deteriorating by the day!

While we should not sound alarmist, we must admit that somewhere along the line something basically wrong has taken roots and is slowly gnawing the system. We cannot blame only the government, but also the socio-religious leaders, the parents and the teachers, for we get the government and the system we deserve. We are all to be blamed for what is happening! Where did we go wrong?

Who is to Blame?

Generally an educational system tries to meet the demands of the times. At some time, with the advent of industrialization and the neglect of small-scale agriculture, our policy makers who mostly reflect the views of the citizens, elaborated school syllabi to meet the needs of industry and the services sector. Rural folks who were eking out a hard but fairly decent living from the farms were attracted by the white-collar jobs of the urban elites who were better paid and who led a cozier life. They wanted their children to have the same life, without realizing what the future had in store for them. Large-scale urbanization started, with the consequent neglect of country life, and giving rise to the parallel squalor surrounding mass-scale production in the industries.

The warped concept of maximization of profits by the owners of the industries led to further demand for workers. They were enticed to earn more and spend more in order to afford luxuries and emulate the Jones next door. The economists encouraged such development, without thinking of the social and psychological consequences of such line of action. Both parents, mother and father, were forced to work in order to meet the family expenses. Children could not receive the attention required for their harmonious development, and were often left to themselves at the mercy of evil influences in the society. Parents were too busy to be with the children, to play with them and help them in their homework, and inculcate in them ancestral good old values that once enriched their lives. Pre-primary schools, nurseries and kindergartens started mushrooming. Personal attention from parents was minimal, and children were the victims of social evils.

For generations this social degradation continued. It's a vicious circle where people crave for superfluous material belongings that they can only acquire by working harder, away from their children. The bane of consumerism is only now being realized by environmentalists who are clamoring for a change in mentality and life-styles. But this change in mentality and life-style will come only when many of our policy makers and leaders themselves give the good example to the public, and our parents and social workers have the capacity to opt for alternative development.

BOX 5: Alcohol in Schools

Alcohol consumption by young and old is becoming a scourge. Parents cannot control their children who consume alcohol in secret, often in the company of others. In a particular secondary school, a young girl, thirteen years old, fell down in class at 10 a.m. She was like in a coma, and had to be rushed to hospital by the school authorities. The doctor found out that she had had an alcohol fit and that she was an alcoholic. Nobody knew for how long she had been taking alcohol. Her parents were urgently called for and they were flabbergasted! With their heads in shame, they took the girl home after some treatment. The school authorities were equally embarrassed and had no alternative than to force the kid to stay at home for some time, just to give a lesson to others who might be having similar problems.

On another occasion, in another girls school, the kids were going for a school picnic, accompanied by teachers. Early in the morning one kid noted some fishy things happening with 'Yoplait' milk mini-bottles, and reported the matter to the headmistress. The latter immediately made a spot check and discovered that eight students had filled their bottles with alcohol in place of milk. They were immediately taken to task and rusticated.

The global trends invariably affect our local situation, and efforts to enforce discipline in schools and colleges have little impact as the external pressure, especially through the global media including the videos and Hollywood and Bollywood films are so strong. But this is not a reason to despair.

Local Situation

Some parents wake up when their own children have taken to the wrong path, become drug and alcohol addicts, and indulge in pre-marital sex or other social diseases that they catch from the media. Instances of children misbehaving and getting caught in the run of diseases and drugs abound. Box 5 gives an instance of how even girls become alcohol addicts at an early age! We tend to believe that boys are the normal delinquents, but with equal opportunities now available to both sexes, girls are as much subject to evil influences as boys.

In another boys school, the head-teacher has been helpless, and has had recourse to police intervention to control boys taking alcohol within the school precincts.

One morning, after the usual assembly, the caretaker noted an odd object hidden up on a tree in the yard. He found that it was a cardboard box, and informed the head-teacher. The latter had it brought down, and was shocked to see that the box was full of beer bottles. He immediately took it to his office and went to convene the teachers for an urgent assembly. Within the few minutes he was out of his office, the entire crate of beer disappeared! He felt ashamed of his students, and called for a special meeting of the Parent Teacher Association. Having heard of the Sukhi Parivaar program, and the talks I was giving to schools and colleges, I was invited to speak on the issue.

On the occasion many parents turned up, and many of them admitted that they had no control over their adolescent kids. As usual, mostly mothers attend such meetings, and they lay the blame on fathers who are themselves heavy alcohol drinkers, or have no time to dialogue with the kids. A lot of convincing is required to get the mothers assume their personal responsibility.

Parents who, for the purpose of socialization, encourage alcohol consumption, have no moral authority to control their own child who later on turns out to be an alcoholic. They should simply ban alcohol from their homes! We can wish them good luck if they can succeed in inculcating restraint and moderation in their children, otherwise.

Abuse of Mobile Phones

At another secondary school where I was invited to talk on value based education and the role of parents, the Headmistress complained openly about the problems she is facing with kids misusing the mobile phones. Pornographic pictures and dirty messages are being sent to other students in class. Short Message Service (SMS) has become a tool for cheating in examinations. The mobile phone enables students to organize secret outings without the knowledge of teachers or parents. Indiscipline is increasing in so many schools, and parents are basically to be blamed for their leniency towards their children, and for sacrificing hard earned money to provide the kids with costly mobile phones that are not essential.

In her own school, the Headmistress has forbidden students to take mobile phones in class, and to hand over the phone to her office in the morning and collect them in the afternoon when they leave school. She hopes similar action be taken in other schools as well.

Children absent themselves from class and parents are not aware of such delinquency. It's only when the police catch them at odd places and call the parents that they wake up to the need for better control. Early sex because of the pornographic films, is becoming a way of life amidst the youth. Teen pregnancies are so common in many countries, and here in Mauritius, this is catching up. Pedophiles are not uncommon, and even some teachers and parents are the culprits! Broken families and early child abuse invariably lead to an increase in prostitution. HIV is on the increase!

There are many cases where students have used **violence against teachers**, and when the teachers complain to the parents, the latter, instead of admonishing their kids, blame the teachers for what has happened! It is such an attitude of parents that encourages the kids to become inveterate delinquents, and criminals in later life.

Need for Sukhi Parivaar Program

Hence the urgent need for the Sukhi Parivaar program through which parents will be encouraged to assume their responsibilities and be able to monitor the development of their children regularly.

The Government can only enforce discipline to a certain extent, but unless it receives the cooperation of the teachers and the parents, and especially the parents, very little can be achieved. Teachers, through their trade unions are asking for greater protection of their members in the face of increasing indiscipline and violence in schools, but they should understand that besides being protectors of the teachers, they should also play their civic role as educators of parents. They can organize talks and courses on parental responsibility, and assist the PTA's in promoting discipline at home and in the schools.

The teacher education programs conducted by the Government should also have a component on parental responsibility, something they can promote in the Parent Teacher Associations, and elements of which they can teach in class. Too much of emphasis on academic subjects with the objective of the students scoring high grades in the examinations, to the detriment of real education, should be discouraged. What is the point of having high-level professionals, individually excelling in their disciplines, but unable to communicate properly and live in harmony with people around? What is the point in having qualified people easily attracted by the easy ways to make money, and thereby abetting and developing corrupt practices that tarnish a society? For sure our parents and educators would not opt for such a society!

Human Values, universally acceptable, should form an integral part of the curriculum. Then only we can produce citizens imbued with the capacity to develop and sustain a humane society with concepts of '**plain living and high thinking'**.

> *'Success is not the key to happiness. Happiness is the key to success. If you love what you are doing, you will be successful.'*
>
> ***—Albert Schweitzer***

Chapter IX

The Crucial Role of Parenting

'If I had My Child to Raise Over Again

If I had my child to raise all over again,
I'd build self-esteem first, and the house later.
I'd point the finger less, and finger paint more.
I would do less correcting and more connecting.
I'd take my eyes off my watch, and watch with my eyes.
I would care to know less and know to care more.
I'd take more hikes and fly more kites.
I'd stop playing serious, and seriously play.
I would run through more fields and gaze at more stars.
I'd do more hugging and less tugging.
I'd see the oak tree in the acorn more often.
I would be firm less often, and affirm much more.
I'd model less about the love of power,
And more about the power of LOVE.

—Diane Loomas'

One of the main objectives of the Sukhi Parivaar program is monitoring the development of the children in the family, and enabling every member to keep track of what is happening with respect to one another. Like in most projects, the success or failure of a project depends on the presence or absence of close monitoring by the project leader/s. The same is the case in families. The responsibility for close monitoring here is in the hands of the parents.

These days, because of the increased pressure on life propelled by the spirit of consumerism, competition, and the urge to earn more, people have little time to devote to basics of self and societal development. Working overtime to earn some extra money, running after new gadgets on the shelves of supermarkets, as publicized in the daily media, accepting night duty when other less paying options do exist, ensuring that one does not miss his/her favorite program on the TV, getting lost in surfing the internet, or the elders attending parties while the family is left to itself, are the norms that dictate most lives these days. Few realize that devoting some quality time with the family has deeper significance, and can contribute immensely to family happiness, much more than greater wealth.

Post-Industrial New Roles for Parents

The role of parents has changed over time due to the way the society has evolved. In the early days preceding the industrial revolution, children grew up in extended families where grandparents, uncles and aunts had a share in the upbringing, and family values were transferred accordingly to the children. After industrialization started, families were forced to migrate nearer to the site of work, and the number of children per family decreased with the advent of nuclear families.[19]

Parental responsibility for early child-care suffered a setback, with the result that internalization of values was marginalized in the face of the race for higher materialistic lifestyles. Now, after seeing what is happening in the society, it is necessary to get back to the basics of parenting, and give as much attention as possible to the role of parents for a happier family life.

A Spirit of Sacrifice Essential

Few realize that by sacrificing some of the superfluous material belongings that bind us more and more to artificial living we can enrich our inner lives all the more! And still fewer realize that having less money in the pocket or less material belongings is less important than the joy and peace we can share in the family! Family solidarity, mutual emotional and material support in an atmosphere of mutual understanding where one is loved and has lots to share are values that can be inculcated mainly through the Sukhi Parivaar program.

The program stresses on regular dialogue within families. It's during such dialogues that parenting can become effective in inculcating values and in changing life styles. Many believe that just providing the children with basic needs, and catering for their schooling and recreational needs are all that is required. Children have different needs at different ages, and understanding them is essential for a proper effort to meet these needs. All needs cannot be fulfilled and children as well as parents have to know the limitations on the resources available for the fulfillment of these needs. We should all learn to cut our coat according to the size of the cloth available, and where necessary to acquire more if the resources permit.

Don't Spoil Your Child

But then, just because we sometimes can afford the extra needs, it is not necessary to acquire them for we must not fall into consumerism, and be aware of global problems like environment, climate change, social disruption, and the like. Consumerism is playing havoc on our environment and life styles. And we have to change our attitude towards our children and the family.

This is where the shoe pinches! It requires a good deal of self-discipline and some peer support. We have to retune ourselves internally to the selective wavebands that are vibrating around, and judiciously select those that can be beneficial to ourselves, our children and the society around. Our emotions have to be balanced with our intelligence and discretion. Otherwise we tend to float with the waves and wreck on the shores or reefs that eventually stop us. Prevention is always better than the cure!

Parenting does not often come naturally, and has to be taught. Natural instincts have to be curbed for the greater benefit of the child. While we do have to lavish love on our children so that they learn to appreciate the same, we must not spoil them by giving in to all their whims and caprices. A measure of strictness is necessary.

Your Eyes can be Enough to Give the Right Signal

The eyes of the parents are very important and must be utilized to let the child know that you mean business. Just a look is enough to make the child understand that he has to change his behavior or face punishment. When the child is still a very young baby, the mother's eyes express both love and displeasure, and this gets imprinted in the child's memory. Later on, just a look is enough to give the necessary notice to the child. But at all times children must feel that they are loved by the parents and others in the family, and that when the parent is strict, that is for his (the child's) benefit.

At times a spanking is necessary to punish the misbehaving child as a last resort. But before that we must try and understand the motive behind the child's behavior. It may be a genuine problem that has to be solved. For this patience is essential on the part of the parent. Then only the child will appreciate that whatever action the parent takes is for his own, (child's) benefit.

Your Child Needs Your Friendship Also

As the child grows up, our attitude and behavior towards him or her has to change also. Up to the age of eight the main emotional support for the children is the family, and parents have to sacrifice their time to devote as much attention as possible to the needs of the child. It is during this period that the child learns most from the parents. From eight to eleven the school teacher has greater influence and from eleven till adolescence ends, friends, teachers and the media have the greatest influence. But this does not mean that parents have no role in shaping the development of the child. Parents should behave like friends and be able to win the trust and confidence of the growing child. They have to find time to play with him or her, and provide help in the homework that the school has given.

During early adolescence children seek to confide in somebody, and parents should be able to win their confidence by being friendly to them. Children then realize that they can have the necessary support at home itself, and not have recourse to immature friends and outsiders.

Charles de Montesquieu said: ' To become truly great, one has to stand with the people, not above them.' Parents must stand with the family and children at any cost.

Sharing House Chores

Parents should encourage children to share in the house chores like cleaning, brooming, washing the car, buying the grocery, helping in the kitchen and in cooking. No work is demeaning. If children are inducted into sharing such tasks at an early age, they grow up to appreciate manual tasks and understand the work of others. They thus learn that all beings do not necessarily have the same talents and the same privileges.

Once in a week parents and children should jointly do the cooking, washing and ironing, and in taking turns in specific tasks. Even if they can afford servants, they should make a habit of doing without any outside help now and then. Then only children learn the dignity of labor and can fend for themselves when required.

Be Liberal with Compliments

Whenever there is a work well done by the child, parents must show their appreciation by complimenting him or her. This helps to build self-esteem in a child, something that is extremely important in the future development of the child. The more we compliment a child for his achievement, the more it increases his self-esteem and willpower to do more and better. And when the work is not up to the mark, instead of rebuke parents must try to understand the child's weak points and provide timely remedy. Rebuke will only weaken the child's ability to strive for better results.

As a child I remember my elder cousin who was a teacher complimenting me on my essays, and remarking: 'Childhood shows manhood as morning shows the day!' That gave me much confidence in myself and encouraged me to do even more and better.

Build Extended Family Ties

In many cultures the joint family system has disappeared. This does not mean that children are to be kept unaware of relatives, wherever they live. Children must be introduced to relatives so that they know that there are other people outside the close family with parents and siblings. Regular visits to these relatives can strengthen the bonds and help to make the children feel secure and loved. These days, because of the growth of nuclear families, many children do not even know their first cousins! It is such a natural pleasure to note that the person we meet is a close relative!

Transferring Values

Universal values like love, respect for others and for all life in nature, forbearance, truth, perseverance, thrift, non-stealing, hard work, firmness, compassion, non-violence, purity of thought and action, control over the senses, acquisition of righteous knowledge, charity and service to others, faith and belief in the immutable laws of nature are some of the main values that have to be imbibed during childhood, and parents are responsible for transferring such values in the children. Teachers and other members of the society also come in but the primary responsibility is on the parents.

How do we transfer these values? The first requisite is that parents themselves must be the role models for children in their early age. They must behave and act in such a way as to give the right examples to the children, and this requires self-sacrifice and self-control. They cannot ask a child to do something that they themselves dislike.

In the course of the daily dialogue parents can give examples of great personalities from history as well as those among contemporary individuals. They can relate the lives of such people. They can read stories depicting such values. And encourage them participate in programs that bear on universal human values.

The Parent's Dilemma

Even if a parent would like his child to adopt good habits and develop a strong character, sometimes he finds it difficult to change his own demeanor. He may have developed a habit of taking much alcohol or cigarettes that are not conducive to health. He may have been abusing of his position to siphon out resources from his firm or office. He may be having extramarital relationships or he may be a habitual gambler. In such circumstances he will not be able to conduct the Sukhi Parivaar program at home as his children or his wife may be aware of these weaknesses. Children always look up to parents for guidance. But here, unless the parents are themselves clear of the above evils, children will never believe them. It is then essential for parents to turn over a new leaf first. Then only they can open themselves up within the family communion. The parent's self-control is the first criterion for the success of the program. At times they may need outside help for changing their habits. Peer pressure has to be resisted. Otherwise the family situation may go from bad to worse. Most crimes are perpetrated by people who have had bad parents.

Good Parents Invariably Make Good Children and Good Citizens

Thus proper parenting is essential to build the full personality of the child. Good and bad characteristics in the child are directly related to the attention we pay to them during their early years of development. Good parents invariably make good children and good citizens. That is why it is necessary for parents themselves to adopt life-styles that enable children to follow them without much pressure from the environment. If we want changes to be effected in our social and physical environment, as Mahatma Gandhi has said, we must ourselves be the agents of these changes. When we fail in our duties, others will have their say and shape the character of our children. That is why the Sukhi Parivaar program, with its stress on continuous monitoring, can be the solution.

As adults we may usually realize our failures later in life. But the present generation and future generations to come will benefit enormously from adopting the program.

Chapter X

Character Building

'The ultimate measure of a man is not where he stands in moments of comfort and convenience, but where he stands at times of challenge and controversy.'

—Martin Luther King

Character building is one of the main objectives of education. An educated person is one who has the capacity to realize himself/herself, earn a decent living and serve his family and the society to improve both their standard and quality of life, in harmony with the environment. People often make the mistake of believing that those with high qualifications are properly educated! While most present qualifications enable a person to have access to higher paying jobs, or a respected profession, they do not necessarily enable the individual to be a better human person. Material progress is only one aspect of human development, a development that has to be in tune with the physical and human environment. Proper education has to cater for the trio of physical, mental and spiritual development.

Our Current Educational System

Of late schools and colleges have been concentrating on 'temporal' education, enabling the individuals to become qualified professionals in their chosen fields.

Western education that has enabled the people to have higher living standards, in fast growing economies, has become the norm. More and more students are taking to commercial subjects, and the intake at secondary and tertiary levels in the humanities and in the sciences is very poor. People want to become rich fast and enjoy the costly amenities of material life. In the process consumerism is becoming another way of life, all the more as industrial manufacturers are spending significant amounts on advertising and marketing their products.

Young people are the first victims of such advertisements as they see them in the regular media, or during their internet sessions, or from role models in their surroundings. They are usually not mature enough to see the sales strategy of the manufacturers, the market specialists and their advertising agencies. A simple gimmick as advertising a product for $ 9.99 is not questioned, when common sense would dictate that there could hardly be any difference if it were advertised for $10.00. Peer pressure is high when home education and values are not inculcated. Parents who can afford usually tend to spoil their children with the latest gadgets and fashions, and those who cannot afford are subject to great pressure by their kids. Stories of parents who get tempted by easy money or have to sacrifice so many essentials just to keep their children happy, abound.

Young couples are also victims of this age of consumerism, as value concepts are changing. In the good old days young couples were encouraged to save for future needs, including education of their children. Now they are encouraged to live fully for the day, and often spend all their earnings on non-essential luxuries.

They get bogged up in borrowing and accumulating bank loans, and end up with blood pressure, health problems and depression, alcohol, suicide, or divorce. Living beyond one's means is the direct outcome of consumerism. Banks encourage this to increase their profits! And manufacturers always think of increasing their sales to maximize profits. As for the pundits of advanced economics, they encourage consumerism so as to spur economic growth!

Satisfying One's Greed

Others who earn well, desire to possess material luxuries more and more. When they are short of means, they are easily tempted by unethical ways of earning more, and corruption starts in their lives. Influenced by the advertisements and peer pressure, they are not content with a small house or a small car, and go for a bigger one. Then they go for holiday bungalows by the lake or the sea. Then they need a boat to sail the waters, after which they want a yacht. Soon they are not satisfied with the yacht and acquire a bigger one! After that they want to possess their own island, and need a jet airplane to travel to and from that place! Their needs are never satisfied as greed has overpowered their natural instincts. That is the path that modern temporal education is promoting. And most parents want their children to acquire such education at any expense, not realizing what harm they are doing to this planet with its limited resources. **Why then should we complain of global warming, and global financial crisis?**[20]

Wise old Mahatma Gandhi had said that there is enough for every person's need but not enough for every person's greed!

Inculcating Truth and Other Values

As children we are taught to speak the truth, and generally as we grow up, gradually we tend to forget what we learnt. We are taught to adapt to changing circumstances that are often man-made. And in the process what we say and what we do are not often in accordance with our own conscience. Our conscience is a mix of instinctive knowledge, and the inner voice and guidance of our creator. In many cases, through repeated acts of self-deceit, guided by lust and greed, we end up killing our conscience, thus paving the way for any form of unethical ventures.

In the Sukhi Parivaar program we ask the children to relate their daily activities, and we are able to monitor their movements and development. They realize that if they lie to their parents, sooner or later they will be caught, and that will strain relations. Hence they learn to speak the truth, and this then becomes a habit and thereby strengthens their character. External pressures forcing them to hide the truth will then not influence them so easily. The earlier in the life of a child this program is implemented, the better it is. The child's overall making and behavior will be gradually molded as required. During and after adolescence, the task is more difficult, and only the parents' patience and perseverance will help.

BOX 6: How Gandhi Taught Truth to His Son

Dr. Arun Gandhi, son of the great Mahatma, relates how he learnt truth from his father.

They lived in South Africa, 18 miles outside Durban. Once Gandhi had to go to the city for conference and asked Arun, 16 years of age, to drive him there, and pick him up at 17.00 hours at a given place. Arun had to buy groceries and get the car serviced meanwhile. After he finished his jobs, he was tempted to see a John Wayne film, where he got so engrossed that he forgot his father. When he got out, it was nearly 17.30. He rushed to see his father waiting. When asked why he was late, he lied, saying the car was not ready, unaware that his father had earlier rung the garage. The Mahatma felt so sad that he had failed in teaching the son to tell the truth. He decided to walk the way back in order to ruminate on where he went wrong in his teachings! For five hours in the dark Arun drove the car slowly behind, watching his father walking in the dirty road, and felt so sorry for not having spoken the truth. This taught him to be true all his life! Had Gandhi just scolded him or slapped him, a usual reaction from a parent, he would not have learnt such a lesson in life. Non-violent action of the father was able to transform him.

Increase in Hypocrisy

Hypocrisy is becoming a way of life. When people do not have the courage to speak the truth, or they want either to ensure their personal gains, or not disappoint the other person, they resort to diplomatic ways of not telling the truth. People then accept this as their normal way of interaction. In some societies, when a junior officer does not agree with the boss, he simply goes to the latter's office and tells him so in a polite way, and the boss respects his views though he disagrees with him. For the enlightened boss, he wins the respect for his frankness. Bosses must be trained to deal with such circumstances. In other societies, the junior officer prefers to suffer alone and fears to risk the anger and reprisal of the senior officer. This eventually leads to frustration and frequent depression. Being frank and courteous at the same time can reduce the suffering of others. The Sukhi Parivaar program teaches one to be frank and empathize with others.

Under such conditions honesty, integrity, up-righteousness, firmness, and value-based characteristics ennoble his or her personality. In a society ridden with a distorted sense of values, such a person may look like the odd one, but his firmness and strength of character will influence others positively.

We keep saying that one must respect the views of the others even if we disagree with them. This is valid when the other person's views do not harm others and the surroundings. By being frank and open to dialogue, we can avoid evil from increasing. The context determines the relative nature of certain cultural practices, but truth that is absolute and universal and is the message of the conscience has to be upheld. This will require a degree of selflessness and regard for the greater good of all around.

The Five Great Weaknesses!

Our sages have said that there are five great weaknesses that we can avoid through character building and the spirit of sacrifice. These are: **Lust, anger, greed, excessive sadness and inflated ego.**

All these perturb the mind, cloud it, and prevent rational decisions. In a way they are another form of madness where the individual loses all self-control, and commits blunders that bring regret at a later period, provided he/she has not killed the inner conscience by repeating such acts. Lust and greed are the very basis of evil in this world. Anger is something common with individuals. We may all have experienced such moments, when, after having lost our temper with others for their wrong deeds or words, we later realize that we should not have reacted in that manner, and feel sorry for it. The achievement of self-control at all moments is a mark of high personal development. That is why it is necessary to practice yoga and meditation that allow the individual to analyze one's self and to reach a level of balance in the personality.

Compassion for others, unlike excessive sadness or pity, is a positive virtue and arises when we understand their problems better. Presently individualism is spreading, and the spirit of sharing and common good decreasing, with consequent loss of regard and compassion.

There is too much attention on individual's rights with less on individual's duties. Value systems are being considered as relative. In the process much harm is ensuing on all life and the environment. The effects of greed are visible through the havocs of consumerism.

Excessive sadness leads to self-harm and physical disorders. And inflated ego is the cause of inappropriate action and harm to others. The inability of an individual to look at a problem from many different angles is the cause of a wrong perception of one's capability, and leads to excessive ego. One can be an expert in one field, but not in everything. The more we know that we do not know enough, the more we become humble, and are prepared to listen and share. Otherwise, through our inflated ego, we tend to destroy rather than construct. I have witnessed such things amidst so many intellectuals!

It is said that the person endowed with truth, charity, fortitude, good conduct, gentleness, austerity and compassion occupies the highest position in the social ladder, even if he is not materially well off. According to Confucius, the Chinese philosopher (551–479 BC), *'To be able under all circumstances to practice five things constitutes perfect virtue; these five things are gravity, generosity of soul, sincerity, earnestness and kindness.'*

These virtues can be promoted, and weaknesses mentioned earlier can be arrested through the Sukhi Parivaar program that teaches all to share their thoughts and jointly participate in solving the problems in the family. It also enables every individual to analyze oneself and avoid the pitfalls of the five great weaknesses. A holistic character building is the direct result of this program.

CHAPTER XI

What We Have to Guard Against

'We are prone to judge success by the index of our salaries or the size of our automobile rather than by the quality of our service and relationship to mankind.'

—Dr. Martin Luther King Jr

The world we live in is a mix of good and evil. The Sukhi Parivaar program may appear too idealistic to many who realize the difficulties experienced in changing mindsets. Many would forget the struggle for achieving higher levels of ethical and moral behavior and go for pure pragmatism, trying to accommodate the changes in lifestyles as we go along. They would surmise that the idealism in the program is utopia! They however forget that whatever positive changes we have witnessed in human civilization have had their roots in our efforts to convert the ideals into concrete practices that are within the reach of the majority. Dreams are realizable provided we believe in them and work for their realization wholeheartedly. Optimism is always a better alternative to pessimism.

The Sukhi Parivaar program will generally benefit the society at large. But it can have a hitch if parents are not open-minded. Our aim is to promote universal values, acceptable to all without any distinction of race, creed or gender. In a way we are aiming at a universal development based on mutual understanding, peace, harmony and sharing of the limited resources we have. However, cultural differences often create a road-block.

The world, alas, is not homogeneous! Glaring disparities in the state of development across the planet have led to internecine and international conflicts. This is daily portrayed by the local and international news, and these days, there is not a day that goes by without some suicide bomber blowing buildings and killing many innocent civilians. In order to maintain economic power, some are not ready to sacrifice their life-styles and allow a greater sharing of the world's limited resources. Changing their life-styles will require their reduction in the use of energy and natural resources. This would mean sacrificing big cars for small ones using minimum sustainable energy, living in smaller houses using environmentally sound energy, consuming naturally grown products, encouraging smaller industries spread over the countryside, and most of all, giving up on luxuries, the mark of high living standards. With the advent of global warming and its negative impact on life, common sense will prevail, but will require time and understanding.

Glaring Disparities, Cause of Unrest and Indoctrination

Sometimes through devious means, some are out to exploit those that do not have the know-how or the means for local development. The under-developed countries are shown the glamour of 'development' and tempted to borrow more and more in the name of economic development and thus get caught in the vicious trap of indebtedness and subservience. Even at the local level in some countries, some wallow in wealth while others have barely the means to survive.

They spend just in one dinner at a restaurant an amount that is often more than a whole month's earning by the man on the street or housemaid they employ. Government allocations to improve the living conditions of these poor communities hardly reach them, and in some countries over ninety percent are siphoned out by unscrupulous so-called educated middlemen. With the advent of TV and the internet, where accessible, these poor see what is happening, and develop growing resentment.

In such a context many rebel groups have sprung up, having taken the struggle on an ideological plane. Such groups are utilizing religious or Marxist doctrines to support their moves, and attracting young people to join the struggle. They offer training to people for guerilla warfare and for extremist actions like suicide bombings. They brainwash the suicide bombers into believing that the doors of heaven are opened for them when they sacrifice themselves. At the same time they ensure that their families will receive compensation and a means of livelihood if they depart.

It is possible that within such groups, parents who have suffered, whose family members have been massacred by rival groups, or the rulers, and who have been brainwashed by peers, can have a different world view of development. And such parents may have no compunction in ensuring that their children follow the same struggle. This is where the danger of indoctrination by the elders of the young members of the family can have a devastating effect. Such parents could support the training of suicide bombers and engage in ruthless war.

In such a context the Sukhi Parivaar program can only promote the evil that the elders nurse, and the children can be easily influenced by the parents to adopt a path of rebellion against the powers that rule. External intervention to bring about a new vision of development with social engagement as the means can make an impact. This will require first and foremost the provision of essential basic needs, and the winning of trust of the local community.

Mercenaries and Arms-Traders

Then there are mercenaries who are intent on amassing wealth by selling all types of arms supplied by countries that believe that arms manufacturing and selling are lucrative ways to maintain their supremacy, GDP growth and higher living standards. Finding ready buyers is a boon for such criminal mercenaries. The trade in arms, official and illicit, is the curse of the present civilization. It is estimated that the global trade in arms amounts to 1.5 trillion US dollars, and this is almost 5% of global GDP which is around sixty trillion USD. The United Nations, in spite of its many declarations, is helpless in such a case, and ruthless crimes and conflicts continue, offering a fertile ground for the training of terrorist guerillas and suicide bombers.

Many leaders in such countries sign the universal declarations at the United Nations, but pay lip service to their adoption. Under pressure from the multinationals pushing for greater access to opportunities to make more profits, they yield to the concept of higher economic growth to sustain development. At the same time, those in power are keen to safeguard their acquisitions, and in the face of growing disparities and discontent, they have to buy new weapons or manufacture them and sell them to other countries for huge profits. The vicious circle of unscrupulous economic growth, higher living standards, and growing disparities chain them to a development pattern that the common man hardly understands.

What Solutions?

The main solution in such circumstances is engagement through appropriate education and provision of basic amenities, through empowerment, for a healthy development. This includes opportunities for gainful employment of the local people. Developed communities have to sacrifice some of their wealth and use it to engage the potential rebel areas in adopting new development paths based on universal values and rational sciences. But the priority should be to meet their basic needs!

Parents in such localities have to be educated first, and their basic needs should be fulfilled. Otherwise jealousy and the feeling of repression and inhuman discrimination will take the upper hand. Both local government and the NGO's have to engage in providing such education to the elders and bring them in line with universal ideas. Their basic needs have to be met as a matter of highest priority; otherwise they may wreck the legitimate process of sane global development.

Adult Literacy Programs have to be Promoted

Schools and colleges have to be opened after normal working hours in order to enable the elders, both men and women, to follow education and training that they missed as children. Local socio-cultural and religious organizations must be provided with standard material for such courses, otherwise they may not be in line with universal values and thinking. Evil traditions and local prejudices can be difficult to overcome, and patience is necessary. *When we realize that eight hundred million people are still illiterate, we can realize the immensity of dangers of evil traditions, religious bigotry and prejudices that have to be tackled.* In the name of culture and religion, many people are ready to lay down their lives. They need to be properly educated so that universal values take precedence over local and regional prejudices.

There is a tendency to believe, by some, that value systems start with Plato or Aristotle. Old cultures have their own sense of values and if they are in line with universal values, they have to be preserved with their own flavor. Culture finds expression in different forms, but the values behind them can be eternal. It is foolish to thrust one's culture over that of others. Medieval beliefs on proselytizing and spreading one form of culture have to be discarded. Rather, it is necessary to ensure that universal values are internalized in different cultures.

Once communities have reached a certain level of education, promoting the Sukhi Parivaar program in their midst will then strengthen bonds for the protection of one another, rather than sustain the spirit of self-destruction, as seen in suicide bombers.

Everybody wants to have a happy life, and when this is not possible because of repression of some by others, with greed and ensuing exploitation as the main causes, dissension, strife, violence and wars are the results. Under such conditions the Sukhi Parivaar program may not work, for parents are not prepared and are tempted to make a difference in their lives through violence. Fulfilling their basic needs along with mass education is a pre-condition and the priority of priorities for a healthy and happy family.

For cynics who will claim that the program is idealistic, and if promoted, will lead to suicide bombers in some societies, we have to assure then that in such societies, preliminary adult literacy and education coupled with meeting their basic needs are prerequisites. Education must have as main objective the adoption of universal human values.

Chapter XII

An Encounter with Parents

'It does not matter how slowly you go so long as you do not stop.'

—Confucius

Parents generally find the Sukhi Parivaar program quite appealing, but they have their own constraints about applying it in their homes. The general issues concern the availability of time, the absence of the other partner, the reluctance of the youngsters to get together, especially if they are over eight years of age, the outside-home environment, and the empathy of decision makers.

I had the opportunity to address a group of parents, some accompanied by their children, at one of our many sensitization campaigns in a remote village in Mauritius. The session was organized by the National Women's Council, in the village community center. It was early in the afternoon, and parents were free before they would have to go and pick their kids from school, or go for preparing the evening meal. Hence, as the main speaker, I had all the time to myself.

After talking for nearly forty minutes, highlighting global and local social problems, like the gradual dismantling of families, and the primary role of parents in educating their children, I opened the session for interaction, with questions and answers. Here is a typical interaction, and a typical Q&A session after a presentation of the program.

Parent: What you are saying is true, but people now have no time for dialogue. We, as parents, have to prepare the food and feed the family. The children have their homework, and are not prepared to stop everything to listen to us. Then we have our favorite TV serial to watch. Each one is busy in his own way. What can we then do?

Speaker: Agreed, we are all busy, but if we do not make an additional effort to communicate with the children, they will turn up as the kids we see on the streets, or as qualified technicians and professionals with no ethical and value orientations, getting easily corrupted, with the result that we will gradually destroy ourselves and the globe. Not being able to find time for communication and dialogue is only an excuse. If you can't do it in the evenings, you can get up early and do it in the morning! It's only a matter of ***willpower***! You are responsible for your welfare as well as for your family. You have the primal responsibility of bringing happiness in the family and around you. Look at the misery around, the global warming we are witnessing. And the global financial crisis we have to cope with.

Parent: What is all that? How does it affect our life here?

Speaker: When we listen to the news or read in the daily papers, we regularly note that in country X or Y there has been an earthquake or a landslide, or a flood, or a prolonged drought and starvation, or a tsunami, or a cyclone, taking hundreds and thousands of innocent lives in their wake. We feel helpless and sympathize with those suffering families, pledging financial and other support for them. We never know when such a catastrophe will strike our own country, our own doors! We say it's an act of God, but do not understand what is actually causing them.

Parent: What is then the cause? Is God angry with us?

Speaker: Scientists have found that our planet earth with its biosphere is like a living entity, suffering from and an ever-rising fever. They call it global warming. This is due to the high amount of carbon dioxide, a gas we release when we burn petrol or carbon to produce electricity for home or for industries, or run our cars, buses or airplanes. The gas forms a layer above the earth and traps the heat radiated by earth like in a greenhouse or a house exposed to sunshine with closed glass doors and windows. This heat is rapidly melting ice caps, raising sea-levels, and causing a change in climate. Winters are getting shorter and summers longer. New diseases like 'chikungunya', H1N1, and others are attacking us. All this is the result of man's activities and are man-made.

An Encounter with Parents
on Sukhi Parivaar

Parent: But we are not responsible for that!

Speaker: Yes we are responsible! I'll give you just one example. We all depend on energy from petrol, gas or electricity. When we leave our lights on even for a minute when we are not there, we are using electricity that is produced by burning fuel. Imagine the amount of fuel consumed globally in our homes, buildings, transport, industries, and the amount of carbon dioxide this is releasing in our atmosphere. It's enormous, millions and millions of tons of this harmful gas! To be more precise, eighty million tons of this CO_2 every day! We are all adding to this global warming by our lifestyles. So it is our duty to teach our children about these, change our personal lifestyles, and this is possible when we ourselves understand the why and wherefore of events and can have regular dialogues with them.

Parent: Our children have to do their homework. We have to get the food ready before our favorite feature TV program. The father is not often there for he has to meet his fiends at the pub, or promote his business. It is very difficult to get everybody together before dinner. Usually we eat at own times, often watching the TV news or a movie.

Speaker: I understand, but we have to make a choice. Either we carry on as we do, leaving others to take care of the problems of global warming, and see our children getting carried away by the social havocs like alcoholism, drugs, suicides, crimes and becoming hardcore individualists, or we have to resolve to make some sacrifice. I did not tell you about the global financial crisis. Did you know that many countries have become bankrupt, and thousands are losing their jobs and struggling to make a living? Do you know that your food prices have gone up? How did this happen?

Parent: How?

Speaker: We have forgotten to inculcate the right values and attitudes in our children. They grow up to become professionals who have no sense of ethics and morality. And when the first opportunity arises, they tend to accept corruption and take devious unethical means to enrich themselves. This is what happened in the US where private firms gave exorbitant perks and salaries to their top bosses, and big banks gave loans liberally and that could not be paid back, and thus became bankrupt. Government had to step in to protect them by injecting taxpayers' money to keep them going and enable them not to dismiss thousands of workers. This problem invaded many countries. Money became scarce, and economic crisis ensued.

Parent: But we are not responsible for that! Our children are good children. They are studying very well!

Speaker: That is not good enough! We are not regularly inculcating into them family and social values like mutual understanding, compassion, solidarity, empathy, moral conduct, and the like. They can study well and eventually earn much, but the core values of living in a community will be missing. The only way you can ensure that is by regularly sitting down with them, dialoging, understanding their problems and themselves understanding your problems. By sharing your problems, joys and sorrows, and by inculcating such values in them, you ensure that they can grow up into socially responsible citizens. They will then look at all beings with compassion and help them, rather than think only of themselves, and grab all that they can to quench their insatiable desires.

Parent: It's a great thing, but requires much sacrifice.

Speaker: Yes, it does require sacrifice. Finding half an hour for the family dialogue in a spirit of communion, without external disturbance, is possible if we can sacrifice some of our pleasures and resolve to improve the family where peace, harmony and love can prevail. It requires sacrifice from ourselves, for we will have to change our habits, the way we talk to our children, the way we help them in their tasks, and the way we look at them as gifts of God that we have to cherish and help them preserve for future generations.

Parent: My children are adolescents, and they do not listen to us!

Speaker: Adolescents have to be treated in a different way. We have to behave as sincere friends with them. In fact they go away from us because they do not find us ready to listen to them. We keep scolding them, and accusing them of this and that. They drift away from us and find solace amidst peers. They require much more patience from our side. Mothers and fathers must try to be friends with them and their friends, invite them home and play with them, organize joint outings with them and share their joys and sorrows. Adolescence is a critical period in their lives when hormonal changes and psychological transformation have a major role in their growth.

Parent: Yes we must organize an outing with them soon, and call all families to spend some time together. We will have fun and bring our children nearer to us!

Speaker: Great! That is the way ahead! But don't forget to get the family before dinner tonight for a Sukhi Parivaar dialogue! Or get up early and find time for such dialogues! If President Obama[21] can find time thrice a week to devote to his family for a dialogue on 'Thorns and Roses', highlighting the events of the day, why can't we?

BOX 7: Global Warming and Climate Change

Our inhabitants on planet earth have known a rapid development using hydrocarbon fossil fuels including coal. This has released too much carbon dioxide in the atmosphere, causing a greenhouse effect and thus increasing the temperature globally. It's like our earth having fever that is increasing more and more! This temperature increase has led to climate changes.

We produce 80 million tons of CO_2 every day! And this keeps increasing! The ensuing temperature increase has led to many catastrophes. While droughts are becoming more destructive, floods in other places are causing landslides and havoc. Cyclones and hurricanes are becoming more severe, while summers hotter and winters colder. These changes are causing new diseases like chikungunya, AH1N1, dengue, with new virus strains to proliferate. Our food production is also affected leading to rise in prices. Poverty is increasing, and sufferance as well.

The global warming has also led to glaciers melting, and sea level rise. This in turn will flood many coastal areas where inhabitants will be affected. Some islands may be completely submerged.

What should we then do? We need to change our lifestyle, consume less fossil fuels, increase production and use of renewable energies, like wind, solar, wave, hydro, geothermal, etc. We should have less airplane travels, use our car less and travel more on foot or bicycle!

More than anything, we should educate people on these changes.

Chapter XIII

Role of Socio-Religious and Socio-Cultural Organizations

While many of our socio-cultural organizations are promoting their culture with a view to keep it alive, and at times struggling to combat specific social disorders, our socio-religious organizations are generally paying less attention to the problems in the society. They are usually busy increasing the number of their adherents, or spending their time in rituals that are other-worldly in substance. They think in terms of after-life heaven or hell, and less in terms of making this world a heaven for all. The abhorring concept of 'us and them' have invaded our minds, divided us and promoted a self-centered philosophy of seeking some advantage or other. If only we could keep our adherents happy by catering to their material and spiritual needs, and ensuring that their children are not going astray, we would be doing justice to the spirit of the founders of the religious societies.

The Sukhi Parivaar or Happy Family program is claiming that if the social evils like alcoholism, drugs, HIV, family violence, suicide, fratricide and the like are not in our homes now, they are at our doorsteps, and will be affecting us soon. Hence preventive measures are essential.

While in developed countries materialism has generally overpowered our way of thinking and living, and people are more concerned with acquiring worldly pleasures and grabbing the limited resources of the earth, in developing countries, the main concern is to increase gross domestic product so that people become richer so as to buy the material commodities showcased by the west. As though they are essential for a peaceful and happy life in harmony with the environment! In the process the many social disorders are fast encroaching in the lives of the people. Heartless inhuman competition is taking a toll on the physical and mental health of the population. The hospitals are bursting with the number of patients, and often there is scarcity of essential drugs. Medical practice, instead of a dedicated professional service, is becoming a business, and the training of doctors is a huge global business! As ailments increase, all around there is a shortage of medical doctors, and medical schools are mushrooming.

Inequities are widening and giving rise to social upheavals where the ruling powers are resorting to increasing the number of soldiers, buying more arms to suppress the dissent and to mass killings to safeguard their privileged positions. Democracies are slowly turning into military states, and neighboring countries are afraid that the disease will spread into their country also. The arms industry is flourishing, and corrupt leaders are filling their coffers with the spoils. Where are our socio-religious organizations? Are they raising such issues in their forum and sending petitions to the powers that be?

Socio-Religious Institutions and Empire Building

Instead of spending their resources on educating the people about their religion and that of others, using modern techniques for the youth, and tackling the social evils, many are busy enlarging their empires.

New temples, new Government subsidized homes, and new bread-earner type 'education' centers are coming up, often thanks to generous Government grants and loans. All of them are expected to increase the incomes of the religious organizations. Erecting new big buildings are their priority, while proper value-based education is being sacrificed for the bread-winner and wealth-enhancer type education modeled on the curricula of the west. Little do they realize that Lord Macauley's objectives are still pursued by revising the curriculum from 'babu' or clerk production to an education that can sustain the industries and life-styles of the developed world, whether in the east or in the west. It is easier to imitate than to innovate.

Character formation that is to be the foundation of any holistic education is, alas, marginalized. Glorification of rituals and the commercialization of religious festivals are increasing, and the gullible semi-literates are falling easy victims of the system. Meanwhile, social problems are increasing. Families are being divided and destroyed. The old people, left to themselves, are being burgled and raped, and have to find shelter in homes that are themselves business enterprises. Governments have to find more and more money to maintain public institutions offering such services, and in some countries prefer, under pressure from capitalists to privatize them. The glory of the welfare state is fast fading!

Instead of just conducting birth, marriage and death ceremonies with their rituals that they hardly explain, all religious organizations, through their priests and religious leaders, should organize pre-marital counseling and training courses (unless they are already doing so regularly), so that the couples understand the true meaning of married life and its obligations. Even during the marriage ceremonies they can explain the necessity of daily communion as in the 'Sukhi Parivaar' program so that couples continue developing the trust and mutual support after marriage.

If socio-religious institutions are to be effective in their vocations, they need to devote their resources to social transformation to ensure a better world with better people, ready to support the weak and the suffering. Government cannot do everything, and relies heavily of socio-religious organizations to give a helping hand in tackling social problems. Instead of building institutions for training humans on better

Sukhi Parivaar Session in Pont Praslin Catholic Center

Living, we build infrastructure for money making! Look at the number of halls that are built just for rentals! And the number of homes for the elderly as it is a lucrative enterprise! We also follow the path of creating a wealthier middle class who can sustain the consumerist system. The number of millionaires and billionaires is fast increasing!

The concept and program of Sukhi Parivaar can make a big difference in our lives and in the development path we espouse. Taking care of the smallest unit of society, the family, with actions that can promote character formation and better citizens, is the only alternative for the effectiveness of socio-religious organizations.

Socio-Cultural Organizations' Roles

As for socio-cultural organizations, they can encourage debates, dramas, shows and programs that highlight family issues and the essential nature of the Sukhi Parivaar concept. They can organize workshops on 'group therapy' an aspect of the Sukhi Parivaar program. They can approach the ministries in charge of culture to have annual competitions and awards to the best families, to families that have the best environment for taking care of their elderly. Schools can have awards for the best parents in their locality. Instead of rewarding only the best students who have distinguished themselves in competitive examinations, they can also reward the best parents whose children have been exemplary in the society, and not necessarily produced the highest mark in the examinations.

Every year we see schools, local communities, local socio-cultural organizations organizing award ceremonies for the best student with the highest mark in the examinations, often with the participation of politicians with whom they want to associate. But we hardly see any event where the best parent or the best family that has kept its elderly well cared and happy, being celebrated. Universal family values should be at the heart of education and development.

The way we live is depicted in our culture. This has to adapt itself over time. While the external representations in culture keep changing, the inner core universal values that characterize a society do not change. This is where the socio-cultural organizations should concentrate their energies. Everything takes its roots in the minds of family members, and this is where the basic work has to start. If the foundations are good, what comes up will most likely be good.

The **United Nations** has declared the fifteenth of May of every year as the **International Family Day.** Socio-cultural organizations need to organize events to celebrate this day in order to awaken interests in the crucial role of parenting and social harmony. We tend to relegate this to the concerned Government Ministry, and this is not what is expected from any society conscious of its role in the community.

When one talks to leaders of socio-cultural organizations, and appeals to them to take a stand against growing social evils, they put the blame on government, and keep saying that examples must come from the top. They forget that they themselves have a primary role in alerting public opinion and effecting a cultural change. One example is the free use of alcohol on certain occasions like the 'chowthari', or the day following a Hindu marriage in Mauritius when close relatives get together to a feast in the presence of the two families whose children have got married. Children often see their parents getting drunk on such occasions. When you request them to stop drinking alcohol on such occasions, they say it is part of the culture! If change has to come, Government should control the selling of alcohol! Little do they realize that such culture can be changed by themselves as responsible cultural organizations giving the lead. They are aware of the havoc this is causing in many families where young men and women get addicted and wreck their lives.

Cultural Centers, besides depicting and promoting ethnic and regional cultures, have to extend their activities to grappling with the ills in society and stressing on the essential role of parents in this venture. Then only the tax-payers' money dished out to them for sustaining their officers would be justified!

Both socio-religious and socio-cultural centers, because of their proximity with the masses, have the capacity to influence both government policies, and effect a change in lifestyles that are in harmony with the global endeavor to maintain peace and harmony everywhere.

A Session in Henrietta, in Presence of Hon. Ministers Sheila Bappoo and Nando Bodha

Chapter XIV

Programs in Schools

Schools normally have Parent Teacher Associations (PTA's) that advise the school management on their orientation. Such organizations can be instrumental in ensuring the success of a program that enables parents and teachers to assume their responsibilities properly. Sometimes teachers do not know the family backgrounds of the students, and parents do not know the problems that teachers face in respect of the students. Discipline in and out of the class is the main issue that forces PTA's to take certain remedial action. But this is not enough.

Community Inputs in the Training

In some countries PTA's even have a say in orienting the school curriculum, in changing it as per the needs of the community in a particular region. They have a say on the management of the schools and in the funding of the institutions also. All is not left to the Government! A certain level of autonomy is essential for enabling local issues to be reflected in the training programs. Decentralization is necessary. Local communities do often raise some funds for some activities, and do not rely solely on the central Government for everything. What is a prerequisite is the enforcement by Government of some basic common programs as per national policies and priorities.

Issue of Discipline

Concerning discipline, these days teachers are required by law not to use physical punishment against students. They can be sued and disciplinary action taken against them. Parents also are told that they should not go against the fundamental rights of children and abuse them physically. They can also be sued by the authorities, either government or NGO's. Sometimes even parents side with their children without having taken due cognizance of the problem, and threaten the teachers. In such an atmosphere, indiscipline gets worse, and delinquency increases. This is where PTA's can be instrumental in bringing about a mutual understanding between parents and teachers with the benefit of the children as the prime motive. They can work on mutually agreed strategies to reduce indiscipline. Many of the problems are highlighted in the chapter VIII on 'What is happening to our kids in schools?'

A Workshop on Sukhi Parivaar in Session

The Happy Family Program

Parent Teacher Associations need first to be made aware of the Sukhi Parivaar or the Happy Family program. This is done by organizing seminars in which parents and teachers have the opportunity to be exposed to the program through resource persons knowledgeable about the program. At such sessions both parents and teachers have the opportunity to raise pertinent questions affecting the behavior and progress of the students. In the presence of qualified experts, they learn how specific problems can be tackled. Often certain problems are brushed under the carpet for fear of the school being ostracized by some people. Such moves invariably add to aggravating the problems. **Sex education** is one such problem amidst conservative communities. And one is aware that with the advent of modern means of communication, lifestyle changes and greater opportunities, children are falling easy preys to bad sexual habits. PTA's must discuss these issues openly in front of knowledgeable people, and find solutions. The program enables such encounters and with the assistance of experts, educates the stakeholders on ways and means to tackle the problems. Drug abuse is another problem that needs urgent attention, as alcoholism is spreading very fast amidst the youth.

Celebrating Family Day

The United Nations has earmarked a particular day in May each year, (15th May) to celebrate the Family Day. This is an occasion to highlight the roles of parents and teachers, and every school should organize a program to celebrate this day. Along with the representatives and assistance of the Sukhi Parivaar program, the schools can organize appropriate events. For example they can celebrate and reward model parents whose children are assets to the prestige of the schools. They can organize special drama shows that highlight the crucial role of teachers and parents in the right development of the children. They can organize essay competitions to bring out new talents and ideas amongst the children, and reward the best ones. These are only a few of the possible programs that schools and PTA's can organize to celebrate the Family Day.

Ministerial Support

Since NGO's are not free to organize programs in Government schools, it is essential for the concerned Ministries to assist, in whatever way possible, the promotion of the Sukhi Parivaar program amidst teachers, parents and children. The existing bureaucracy is often so tenuous and elaborate that getting a permission to introduce the program in a school can take very long. The positive impacts of such programs must first be appreciated by concerned authorities.

Within the curriculum there is urgent need to introduce a component of values-based family participation, if we want to prevent the deterioration of family values in our society. The authorities need to involve the NGO's working in this area to work out a suitable curriculum, and promote this curriculum in the schools. Academic achievement as presently accepted, is not the alpha and omega of education! A holistic view of life and its human presence in the universe is essential for happiness, peace and prosperity.

Otherwise we will train brilliant professionals whose main aims are to make money and enjoy life, abusing of the bounties of Nature.

CHAPTER XV

Some Interrogations: An Appeal to Our Conscience

> *'The world is a dangerous place not because of those who do evil, but because of those who look on and do nothing.'*
>
> ***—Albert Einstein***

Mahatma Gandhi, recognized universally as the 'conscience of mankind', in one of his last notes before he was assassinated, as a reflection of his years of social action, said the following:

> 'Whenever you are in doubt, or when the self becomes too much with you, apply the following test. Recall the face of the poorest and weakest man you may have seen, and ask yourself if the step you contemplate is going to be of any use to him. Will he gain anything by it? Will it restore him to a control over his own life and destiny? In other words, will it lead to swaraj (self government) for the hungry and spiritually starving millions? Then you will find your doubts and your self melt away.'

If only our world leaders and followers had paid enough attention to these words, we would not have witnessed the environmental and social calamities we see and hear about on a daily basis!

Our conscience is dominated by habits we have acquired from childhood and by the norms we have adopted in a society through religious beliefs and through manmade laws. This society is always in a flux with global changes affecting us daily. Many of these changes are often the outcome of concerted deliberations and recommendations at the level of the established international organizations, mostly controlled by economic and political leadership. While the norms are a mix of political and religious convictions, and are subject to change with time and space, there are certain underlying eternal ethical, spiritual and material laws that cannot and do not change. These are the laws that govern our universe, and the understanding and adoption of which determine our attitude to life and our innate conscience. By repeatedly flouting these eternal laws, many have in a way killed their conscience, smothered their inner voice, and are prepared to go to any extremes to fulfill their greed and lust for power and pelf, or to preserve their privileges, often in the name of man-made religions.

Today humanity is paying the price for such life-styles as are destroying the very fabric of society and the physical and social environment. This is what goads me to some fundamental interrogations, the outcome of my own life experiences and observations in different parts of the world. Some may find themselves liable to answer these interrogations, especially if they want to see their own children and the future generations live a better life, in harmony with the laws of nature, with universal happiness as the ultimate objective. To some such interrogations may look naïve, and out of the commonly held views.

But our life is an ever-changing phenomenon, with constant review of our own selves. I think these interrogations may goad us to look within and undertake this review. Such review can be possible and have its impacts when we have regular interactions with our family members and aim at achieving overall happiness. We can then bring in context what is happening outside and at home.

Let us start with these interrogations!

Maximizing Profits and Dismissing Staff

In this business driven world where everything seems to be weighed at the alter of mammon, are we justified in laying off people struggling for a livelihood just to maximize our profits and maintain our lifestyles, while threatening to close down the factories? We can fall back on existing labor laws to say there is nothing illegal, but have we given a humane look at these laws? We have recourse to nominal compensations, voluntary retirement schemes, and a host of means to ensure that we do not go bankrupt, lose our prestige and suffer in the eyes of the people. At the same time we often transfer our previous profits to more lucrative enterprises. Are we morally justified?

At times, back in office, we agree to lay off workers so as to keep the companies competitive or not reduce our own lifestyles. Are we morally justified in doing these? Only recently in the US some top executive directors of Ford Motors had the spirit to dismiss so many workers, and then, with their begging bowl, fly in their private jets to attend the Senate and canvass for government bailing them out through economic stimulus packages. What has happened to our conscience?

In many European countries that are going bankrupt in the context of the global financial crisis, hundreds of thousands of workers are being laid off because of the mismanagement of others. Should we not reduce our own perks to assist these bread earners?

Exorbitant Salaries and Perks

Are we justified in paying ourselves exorbitant salaries and giving ourselves so many perks, while the worker down the ladder is just scraping a poor livelihood? Very often the worker is bogged in debts as a result of struggling to educate his children or paying for their health and food. Are we aware of the miseries of these poor people? Have we ever cared to visit their homes to see how they live? Very often one salary of the boss or those who toe his lines is equivalent to a hundred fold the salary of the poor worker, if not much more. And if we add the money worth of the perks, the amounts are mind-boggling! The British Petroleum boss who was accused of mismanaging the Mexican gulf catastrophe in 2010 received an indemnity of more than 1.2 million Euros, along with a pension of 700,000 Euros per year! This can give us an idea of his monthly salaries. Do we really care for the poor? We usually wallow under the illusion that we are smarter, work harder and deserve what we give ourselves!

Higher Life-Styles, Bigger Homes and Bigger Cars…

Do we realize that our high life-styles based on surrounding ourselves with costly material goods become a benchmark for others to emulate? Do we realize that such lavish living is adding to consumerism and fast destroying the environment and increasing global warming with all its associated negative impacts on life? Are such lifestyles compatible with the age-old wisdom of 'plain living and high thinking'? We sometimes tend to make an ostentatious exhibition of our material grandeur, forgetting that when we die, all the wealth will not accompany us. In a particular country one of the richest men there celebrated the wedding of his child way up in the air, with a Jumbo plane load of invitees enjoying the very best of food and drinks! Was he conscious of the impacts of such lavishness on the country and its people? The very country where eons of social discrimination and inequities have sapped the spirit and lifeblood of teeming millions?

Just because we can afford it, it does not necessarily mean that we should spend it on trivialities or on anything the market advertises! We are often attracted by the big petrol guzzling cars. Can't we do with more modest ones that can take us around safely?

Mother Theresa has a word for them if they care to listen to the voice of their conscience.

> *"At the end of our lives, we will not be judged by how many diplomas we have received, how much money we have made or how many great things we have done. We will be judged by 'I was hungry and you gave me to eat. I was naked and you clothed me. I was homeless and you took me in.'"*
>
> ***—Mother Teresa***

Frequent Air-Travels and Expensive Holidays

Do we realize that for every air travel we make (often enjoy!), we add to the pollution and the concentration of carbon dioxide in the atmosphere, things that are killing our blue-green planet? Should we not limit our air travels to the minimum, and encourage video conferencing where available? These days we have moved further ahead in the realm of internet virtual conferencing, with the development of telepresence in virtual boardrooms where one can move in and out as in real boardrooms. This is being recommended so as to reduce air travel and diminish carbon footprints, and thus positively affect global warming and climate change. We often make people believe that our travels and official missions are for the benefit of our institution and our country. Sometimes it is necessary to be facing one another and study the body language of the other person, or pay our respects to top people, and under such circumstances air travels and face to face meetings cannot be avoided.

As far as holidays overseas are concerned, there is need to restrict the numbers, and not copy those in developed countries who every year plan trips abroad just because they can afford it at present. Our young people are also being led into this lifestyle. Do we realize that one such expensive holidays or official travels could have enabled a low paid worker and his family to live a more decent life with basic amenities for at least a month? However, when we undertake such travels to meet our parents or family members living far away, such trips cannot be avoided.

Daily Subsistence Allowance (DSA) and Hotel Charges

Many officers never miss an opportunity to travel and pocket most of the daily subsistence allowance, or spend it in living in top hotels. It is a status symbol! Often what they spend in one night is enough to pay the liftman, the attendant or the guard for a month! In some countries, just outside the magnificent hotels lie the slums and shanties where the poor workers live. How can our conscience allow us to ignore all that and move around with blinkers, rushing in and out in big cars. We ignore the poor around, consoling ourselves by the delusion that it's their fate!

Some religions and philosophies have even sanctified such beliefs! Are they compatible with modern concepts of mass emancipation, and empowerment of the poor?

Restaurant Dinners and Lunches

Lifestyles are changing and on weekends it is becoming a tradition in some societies not to cook at home and to eat out. We take our families out for lunches and dinners, not on special occasions but for some, almost every weekend. I am sure they would have derived much more happiness involving the entire family joining hands in preparing different dishes at home, and relishing their own creations on some weekends. Once again the amount we spend on such eating sprees could have catered for the month salary of the poor worker there! We tend to pay a salary of pittance to our housemaids who toil to keep our home clean, cook our food, and often look after our kids when we go out at night. Do we stop to question ourselves about our spending sprees, just because we earn higher salaries and can afford luxuries? When some of them commit suicides as they cannot cope with life, we blame the authorities, not ourselves. When others commit burglaries and other crimes trying to sustain themselves, or take to terrorist actions, we hunt them down. The number of such people is increasing when our economic policies should have enabled another scenario. Do we really care?

Some believe that because they enjoy the power of position and money, they can allow themselves to go to excesses. On the open platform they will shout for fraternity, equality and what not, but in their private lives they practice something different. Should they not look into themselves?

Destroying the Planet with its Biodiversity

Our 'development' has led to destructive planetary changes that are not ensuring sustainability. The future generations will possibly not witness the flutter of colorful bees, birds and butterflies that are fast disappearing because of encroaching populations, ever greedy to consume the limited resources available. In thirty years we have destroyed half the forest, the equivalent of thirty-three football grounds per minute! Biodiversity is badly threatened worldwide. In a 'paradise island' like Mauritius, where the dodo was once king, 98% of biodiversity on land has disappeared, and marine biodiversity is now disappearing fast.

If we are not careful, we will also not hear the babble of the brooks, or the laughter of small children. Grown-ups and the elderly are becoming more and more solitary, often left to end their lives in 'homes'. People seem to be running after material comforts, eager to live their personal lives, forgetting their parents, unmindful of the preservation of nature and the environment.

Are we conscious of the harm we are inflicting around us with the type of development we have espoused? Can we look into ourselves and resolve to change for the better, with much greater regard for all life on this planet?

Place of Sukhi Parivaar

These are only a few of the glaring interrogations. You may ask what all these few interrogations have to do with the concept and practice of Sukhi Parivaar.

These interrogations form essential elements of the Sukhi Parivaar program, for unless we discuss them in our families and resolve to face them, the changes that we witness will wreck our lives. After everyone has shared his/her day's experience, we have to take time to discuss the different interrogations. This will force us to look beyond ourselves and become aware of the way people are living and doing things without thinking of others, less fortunate ones. The program offers an opportunity for one and all, young and old, to share their life and jointly plan for a better one. Unless we start in the home, the daily chores of work, study, and recreation will overpower us, and we will get caught in the train of usual 'development'.

CHAPTER XVI

The Risky Future of Humanity

'In all life one should comfort the afflicted, but verily, also, one should afflict the comfortable, and especially when they are comfortably, contentedly, even happily wrong.'

—John Kenneth Galbraith

The scientific facts we have today already forestall global catastrophes in the making. Already we are reaping the bitter fruits of our actions that are causing major climate change impacts on the globe. Can we stop the impending death sentence in time?

We cannot afford to be complacent about the outcome of the United Nations Copenhagen Climate Summit held on 7th to 18th of December 2009. The pronouncement of our leaders at the summit had been remarkable, just as that of the small island of Maldives. Yet few people realize that humanity is at risk and we are fast moving towards a global catastrophe, unless drastic measures are adopted globally!

Besides major disastrous climatic impacts on our environment with impending food, water and environmental crisis and havocs, eighteen of the world's professional medical organizations claim that we are also heading for a global health pandemic.

Global Warming, Climate Change and Impacts

Climate change due to global warming is the biggest issue facing mankind today. This is because of the devastating effects of this phenomenon on a planetary scale, all caused by mankind's unsustainable development paths. Millions of lives are at stake, including ours.

It is recognized that the last Copenhagen Summit was a failure as developed nations could not agree on the assistance they need to provide for saving the planet from further global warming, with related climatic changes. They only agreed on the need to limit global temperature rise to a maximum of two degrees Celsius by 2020.[22] They however recognize that they now have to change their lifestyles, consuming less fossil fuels, and enhancing the production of new and renewable energy from the sun, wind, wave, rivers, geothermal, and bio-fuels. Globally we are producing less than 20% of our needs from renewable sources.

Present Situation

The earth has already registered significant temperature increase (between one and two degrees Celsius) that has caused major catastrophes in different parts of the globe. These days while Asia is experiencing severe floods, Russia is suffering from a heat wave that is devastating huge forests and affecting the lives of millions. At the same time severe hurricanes are affecting parts of the United States, and cyclone prone regions are in danger of very damaging climatic disturbances. Coastal regions will be badly affected by sea-level rise, and while some islands will just disappear from the earth surface, flooding will cause huge devastation to coastal towns and cities. By the end of this century, sea level rise is predicted to be 59 centimeters. Bangladesh and other places will be badly affected.

Food production has already been badly hit and price rises are everywhere. New strains of microbes and viruses have appeared and health authorities are under severe strain. Poor countries with huge populations are the most affected, along with young children and old people who have less immunity to fight diseases. All this is the result of our having accepted a development pattern based on the models of the developed nations where concentration of industries and manufacturing enterprises are gobbling massive amounts of fossil fuels.

We need to realize that this development pattern is releasing **80 million tons of Carbon dioxide daily**, and this keeps increasing. While only a quarter of this is absorbed by the oceans, the rest is responsible for a 'green-house effect' that is increasing the temperature of the earth. Even a two degrees rise in temperature means that 375 million people on the globe could be affected by climate related disasters by 2015.[23] What are the effects of this on human, animal and plant life around?

Just an increase of 1.5 to 2 degrees Celsius in global temperature (we are very near it!) will lead to a loss of 20-30 percent of world species that will die because of lack of proper food or because of natural calamities. There will be a mass movement of plants and animals northward to more temperate new zones, entailing new adaptation problems, and massive costs. 'The earlier we act, the less costly it will be,' says Nicholas Stern, the British Adviser to the Prime Minister. The International Organization for Migration will have a difficult task coping with the mass of migrants, while birds and animal species will fight for their own survival.

Loss to Biodiversity

The overall loss in biodiversity (animals, plants, birds, insects..) will be enormous. Human development impacts on nature will compound this loss. Already we have lost two-thirds of earth species by destruction of forests that were the source of food, energy and raw materials for creatures living there. Within the last thirty years we have destroyed half of the existing forests, the equivalent of 33 football grounds per minute! All this to allow humans to encroach further, building houses, towns, dams, highways and mining! And the devastation continues! Destruction is the other name of civilization!

In the southern hemisphere, an increase in temperatures will also increase the sea temperature, and marine life will be affected. Coral bleaching has been noted as the concentration of CO_2 in sea water, and hence its acidity, increases. This affects fish population consequently, and decreased fish production ensues. It is said that maintaining CO_2 levels as at present will require thousands of years to bring back the ocean acidity to pre-industrial levels.

Increasing Food Crisis

With climate change and its ensuing severe droughts or severe floods or severe winters, food production has already been badly hit. Food prices have been rising and many parts of the world, especially within the African continent (Ethiopia, Sudan, Uganda, Mali....) have experienced starvation as people had no money to buy food. Along with wheat, corn and maize also will have decreased production.

In Mozambique, and elderly woman has this to say: 'The weather has changed a lot. In our time there was the cultivating season, the rainy season, the time for sowing and harvesting, but now it can rain, we sow our seeds, we get so far, then the rain stops and everything dries.'[24] Even Russia where forest fires are still raging (August 2010), and millions of hectares with plantation around villages are burning, the cereal crops are drying, and world wheat prices are bound to go up, as Russia could stop export of wheat for some time so as to meet its own requirements. As a consequence of the destruction of agriculture in rural areas, migration to urban areas will follow. No doubt the poor and the weak will suffer the most.

Increasing temperatures also give rise to proliferation of harmful insects, and this will require greater use of pesticides that affect the environment. Even unwanted weeds will increase. Agriculture will thus be badly hit.

Implications on Health

When it comes to diseases, extremes of heat and cold pose serious risks to older people, as their immunity is weaker with age. Those especially with heart problems will be at greater risk. The rising temperatures will bring an increase in mosquitoes and malaria, chikungunya and dengue fever as new viral diseases that thrive in warm temperatures. In parts of Kenya a seven fold increase has been noted a decade ago. Also water borne diseases are likely to increase. A higher increase in salmonella poisoning and cholera is again a real threat.[25]

As temperatures rise in the northern hemisphere migration of bacteria and viruses will follow, thereby leading to the North experiencing malaria, dengue and other diseases now in the South. Africa and parts of Asia have been struggling with these crippling diseases for centuries, and multinational pharmaceutical companies have still not succeeded in eradicating them and in providing the basic malaria treatments to millions. There was much drum-beating on new and cheap miracle treatments for malaria by researchers, but the fall out on the poor south has been minimal. Perhaps when the North will experience the spread of the disease, much will have to be done and the poor will benefit.

Until the catastrophe strikes at our own doors we will not wake up! Business as usual can no more be the norm! A drastic change in both our vision of development and in our life-styles is required. We should stop having the feeling of 'Ce n'est pas demain la veille!', i.e., it's not tomorrow the eve of complete destruction. Irreversible damages to natural ecosystems, biodiversity, and to agriculture are already visible.

Towards Zero, then Negative Carbon Emissions

Under pressure from proponents of fast economic growth to ensure adequate employment opportunities and sustained life-styles, we have believed that a rise of global temperature to a maximum of 2°C above pre-industrial levels is tolerable. Global greenhouse gas emissions by being reduced by 50% below the 1990 levels could enable us to reach global equilibrium temperature of up to that maximum, acceptable. But the State of the World 2009 report warns us to plan now 'to get back below 1°C as fast as possible by a target of zero carbon emissions going negative' Otherwise we are heading for a sure death sentence on humanity!

Have our development programs stressed on the dire need for ensuring that atmospheric carbon dioxide concentrations stay below the prescribed 350 parts per million? Have we made a scientific study of the volume of carbon dioxide our life-style releases daily? Are we aware of the growing acidification of our seas due to global warming, and the slow disappearance of our corals and other marine life-forms? Have we adopted a low-carbon economy life style? What do our legislations dictate? What are our schools, colleges and media-programs promoting in the area of sustainable lifestyles? These are the issues we need to tackle urgently at the national and global levels.

Mauritius and Small Islands

Global warming will affect everyone to varying degrees. In Mauritius, the flourishing Tourism Industry with the multitudes of top-class hotels on the seacoast, will be badly hit, and may just disappear from our economic map. It is our duty to prevail over the global players, especially those from the developed countries, to allocate substantial resources to enable us take the appropriate preventive measures to avoid such catastrophes. There is a sense of awakening amongst them. They do realize that they are the real culprits leading the world into a pattern of consumerist development that is not sustainable, and that has already caused so much harm to our blue planet. Their timid support at the Copenhagen Summit will not take us far enough.

Green Technologies for All

China and India with their huge populations, are often cited as future rogue countries with respect to environment and sustainable development. It is natural for them to envisage a better standard of living for their people, and this will require heavy demands on energy production and consumption. How can developed countries urge them to adopt environmentally sound technologies without providing them with the necessary resources to buy them and to develop their own? Why not make such technologies non-proprietary? Why can't we promote green technology enterprises with job opportunities for all? All this will demand a heavy investment from those who have contributed to the present global warming. Simultaneously, developed countries should hasten their development and application of green technologies.

A New Development Path

It is possible for humanity to change direction and go for a new economic development path that will stress more on the quality of life than on the standard of living. Our biosphere, in a way, is unique. It is up to us to understand our place in this cosmos, and to take such measures as will ensure that our progeny will be proud of us!

It is important to realize that our planet, its people and profit-craze are three fundamental parameters that have to be harmonized so that sustainable development can be ensured. While profit motivation is the objective of most enterprises, greed should not be the motor. We must know where and when to stop and let the planet breathe! The regular global catastrophes we experience should force us to think differently.

Urgency of Change in Lifestyle

All these point to the need to adopt new lifestyles where we consume less fossil fuel, develop and use more renewable energies, and generally reduce our consumption of natural resources. We should be prepared to sacrifice many of our luxuries in order to ensure a sustainable livelihood for this and future generations. We should travel less by car and plane, use bicycle and other modes of communication. We should opt for smaller cars using renewable energies like biofuels. And promote smaller industries using locally produced energies and empowering the people rather than enriching the rich. It is essential to appreciate that enhancing the quality of life is better than increasing the standard of living.

In a new development paradigm, governments and multinationals should aim at promoting industries and enterprises that are not energy intensive, and energy gobbling. In line with the philosophy of Mahatma Gandhi, John Kenneth Galbraith,[26] Ernst Frederic Schumacher, and others, we should see smaller units of production spread all over the countries, empowering the masses and not the rich, rather than large concentrations in certain areas of the countries. This will have the advantage of using less and locally generated energy from renewable sources like wind, water, biomass and sun, providing jobs to the local people and avoiding their migration to urban areas where the problems of housing, pollution and survival become pronounced. People should understand the negative impacts of affluence and concentration of wealth in the hands of few while others wallow in poverty, the fertile ground for strife and violence. This goes against, what Galbraith called, 'conventional wisdom', that mainstream economists dislike!

Sessions on Sukhi Parivaar Program

Public sessions on the Sukhi Parivaar program make it a point to highlight the above issues and alert public opinion on the need to change their personal lifestyles so that others can follow. Like the small sparrow in the story of the forest fire in Chapter III! For family happiness is invariably linked with global developments, and we cannot ask our children to desist from adopting lifestyles that are common when they are not conscious of the damage being done to our planet, and the real cause of the multiple catastrophes we witness on the daily television screen.

Discussions on what is happening and the possible causes should also take place when we have home sessions of the program. When we can first affect mind-change in the family, we can then experience the same in the society. And it is easier to educate and influence directions in a small group than in a large one.

Optimism, individual and collective commitment to the program should be the guiding force for such a future where all can be happy.

> *"We have to make a choice. Will we obey the market laws of corporate greed or Gaia's laws for maintenance of the earth's ecosystems and the diversity of its beings?"*
>
> **—Vandana Shiva**[27]

Chapter XVII

The Quest for Happiness

'Happiness is when what you think, what you say, and what you do are in harmony'

—Mahatma Gandhi

Everybody is in the search for happiness. Thousands of books have been written on this subject that has given rise to different religions and philosophies over the ages. Many paths have been suggested. The one that stands out is the path of righteousness through right action, the acquisition of sufficient wealth, the controlled and just enjoyment of that wealth, and thereby the enjoyment of happiness in this world and thereafter. The stress is on the **means** that in this case is righteous action. It is through righteous action that we have to acquire sufficient wealth that we enjoy by sharing it with others, and that leads us to happiness. Righteous action is one that is based on ethical and moral values that require that we should not harm others, and that whatever we do has an impact on alleviating the miseries of our neighbors and the world. We should not be content with action that is selfish, but have regard to all living and non-living entities in nature.

Many prescribe that happiness is a state of the mind, and can be found only within oneself, and not necessarily through contact with the outside world. However, as long as our senses are active and we experience what is around us, saying that happiness is within us only can be misleading. Yoga and other disciplines prescribe the control and abstraction of all senses, with focus on the mind, but such states are temporary, and the moment we come out of our contemplation and face reality around and do not ignore this reality, we are back to level one! Some even question the notion of reality and interpret the world as an illusion! Yoga does however help us to train the mind and the body to adopt certain mental and behavioral strategies. Hence the quest for happiness goes on.

The final objective of every activity, whether altruistic or selfish, is some happiness for the individual as a member of the society. For most individuals, personal happiness based on some measure of self-fulfillment is a priority, but for a few exceptional beings motivated by love and service to all, it is the happiness of others that is their priority. Again for many, real and lasting happiness can only be found in heaven where their eventual salvation will take them. On earth, at best, they can only hope to have some moments of temporary happiness.

History has seen some exceptional individuals who sacrificed their lives for the happiness of their fellow beings, and who left a lasting impression on the minds of humanity. Their followers set up different schools of religion and started preaching with a view to share the happiness they found in their practice. Many of their followers even started adoring them as demi-gods or gods, forgetting that the Universal Spirit that pervades all cannot be contained and limited within one mortal. Those exceptional individuals are known as great souls who came to take humanity away from the evil and on a right path. Most of them have been martyrs. One such exceptional person has said:

'I am not concerned about my salvation. I am more concerned about the happiness and salvation of those poor, weak and suffering masses whose misery I have to alleviate. I will attain salvation only when they would have attained theirs!'[28]

Different Philosophies and Paths to Happiness

There seems to be three distinct paths to happiness, all based on the individual's personal environment, training and inclinations. His/her genetic predispositions along with attitude to and involvement in life dictate the type and level of happiness that can be experienced. One path is centered on the individual self; the other is centered on action and service, and the last around complete devotion and surrender to a great soul. Most people try to find the right balance between the three of them, and adopt different degrees of some or all, depending upon their own inclinations.

As members of a family our development and acquired inclinations depend on our preliminary upbringing within the family. If there is peace and harmony within the family, and regular dialogue between the members in a spirit of family communion, the path to happiness becomes easier in a buffeted world.

The Path of the Self

Many believe that happiness can be found only by concentrating on the ego-centered happiness of the self, for if the self is not aware and awake, and the mind is not functional, our experience of anything around is not possible. Everything around us exists only when we can experience its presence through our five senses of sight, hearing, smell, taste and touch. And these eventually are linked to the mind that interprets the experiences and the feelings. When the mind is 'dead', then we cannot experience any happiness! And we are dead. But the fact is that even if we do not exist, the world does, and others do experience any state of happiness or sufferance. Most often our own happiness is invariably linked with the happiness of others. Ego-centrism and extreme individualism, a disease of the materialist world, and also of the atheist, is spreading and in its wake, causing serious harm to mankind and our planet with its biodiversity. Global warming and climate change are examples of this harm. By nature humans are gregarious and survive only in communities, as thinking beings. Otherwise they die out.

We are now in the realm of high philosophy! Wasn't it Rene Descartes who said: 'Cognito ergo sum, or Je pense, donc je suis, or I think therefore I am!'[29] This has to do with being aware of oneself, of one's role and capacity, and of one's state of mind that dictates one's feelings of happiness or suffering. However, whether we are there or not, others are there and do experience such states of their own. Thinking alone is not enough unless these thoughts find expression in some form or other.

The Path of Action

The other path of happiness that is centered on action and service is perhaps the culmination of a civilized being who is conscious of the individual's duty towards the self and the surroundings. This is the path that the majority of mankind prescribes and adheres to. All worthy human achievements are the results of people interacting with others and affecting their varied states of happiness, often in a spirit of pure selfless service and sacrifice. In this path some philosophies have prescribed action without the hope of any immediate reward. For, while we have control over our actions, we do not have control over the time and nature of the reward. It's like somebody having a bow and arrow in his hand, and is going to shoot the arrow. As long as the arrow is within the bow and under his control, he is master of the potential action, but once he releases the taught string of the bow, and the bow is off in air, he has no control over it. So many unknown factors may affect the final destination of the arrow and the time it can hit or miss the target. That is why action with a determination but in a spirit of selfless service is recommended.

Science has perfected the action to such an extent that we are now in a position to determine with great accuracy the impact of that action. We are able to send satellites and rockets with nanosecond accuracy, but there still is an element of mathematical probability that cannot guarantee the full success of the goal. While in theory perfection is possible, in practice the laws of probability are fundamental. It is the same with absolute happiness.

The Path of Devotion

The third path in the quest for happiness mentioned above is that of pure devotion to some superior power, sometimes leaving the very decision to act in the hands of the latter. It is a complete surrender to the will of the superior power. In such a state people usually live without worry, leaving everything to the higher being. Sometimes they get so engrossed in the surrender that they become oblivious of the world around and act as in a trance. They strongly believe that the Creator will take care of them in any circumstance, and thus they stay happy, or at least claim to be so. This concept of happiness may lead to fatalism in which the individual self has no role in what happens in the world around. Evil is tolerated as the other side of the coin. Even destructive self-indulgence is at times attributed to the will of the Lord. The question of will-power then does not arise.

Such attitudes have led to the belief that everything around is an illusion, and the whole of existence is also an illusion. Hence happiness could also be an illusion! And the people who subscribe to such concepts could also be illusory. Moments of depression or inflated self-awareness can be the cause of such outpourings, and we have to be careful in blindly following such beliefs.

Gandhi's View on Happiness

On a more mundane and practical plane happiness is the result of conscious concordance in thought, speech and action. When these are in harmony and one does not contradict the other, happiness is the result. The intentions have to be pure and the speech and action that follow the intentions have to be righteous. This harmony requires much self-control and sacrifice as prerequisites. People who adopt this have to go through long self-preparation and often show much bravery. That is why Gandhi stressed on the harmony between thought, word and deed.[30]

For the majority of people life is a mixture of both happiness and sorrow, but at different times. Complete and lasting happiness is rare. The love that is shared in a family is one of the most important factors that determine happiness. Besides disease and hunger, material needs are the constant causes of unhappiness, while love, mutual trust and understanding with solidarity are the sine-qua-non for happiness.

Our Present Trends

These days many people believe that wealth can lead to happiness. They encourage people to work very hard, be competitive in producing goods and services for the market, increase the gross domestic product and the bank balance, and enjoy the material benefits. In the process many work long hours and have no time for themselves and their family. The 24 by 7 model is being promoted where the economy runs 24 hours in a day and 7 days in the week. In such cases the pressure of work in a competitive environment is such that young people develop blood pressure problems early, and are not ready to get married, settle down and have children who can ensure a continuation of the family. The problems of an ageing population and the need for imported labor in many developed countries are telling on the world economy.

Social science research has been able to quantify well-being and quality of life.[31] In a well-researched paper by Diener, Emmons, Larsen and Griffin published in the Journal of Personality Assessment, it has been shown that money does not necessarily bring happiness, as is well known in the French edict 'L'argent ne fait pas le bonheur'. Countries and people who give more importance to social relations rather than material benefits have registered much higher scores in life satisfaction, and are happier. Developed countries where democracy and market economy dominate, where purchasing power, living standards, material comfort and consumerism are the norm, the measured level of satisfaction has not been any higher than in poorer economies. This is known as the ***Easterlin paradox***, proposed by Easterlin who took Japan as a model.[32] Also, believers in God have a higher score than non-believers! That is how it has been found that people in countries like Latin America and India are comparatively happier with higher levels of satisfaction than those in developed economies. But the sad thing is that our present educational system encourages people to move towards a western lifestyle, unmindful of the social and environmental problems it creates.

If only we could realize that we need to limit our needs, to slow down, have a more balanced economic development with much stress on social issues, and measure development through our taking stock of the 'gross national happiness (GNH)' rather than the gross national product, we would be nearer to a stable happy society.[33] In Bhutan the Prime Minister Lyonpo Jigmi Y. Thinley is known to have said: "The four pillars of GNH are the promotion of equitable and sustainable socioeconomic development, preservation and promotion of cultural values, conservation of the natural environment, and establishment of good governance."[34] This is probably what the world should go by in order to alleviate the ravages of global climate change!

Scientific Research on Happiness

Happiness has mainly been the subject of philosophy and religion, but of late, with the evolution of psychology as a science, scientific observations through research have been made and published in scientific journals.[35] Scientific American published an article by Maria Krakovsky in March 2007 on the work of Sonja Hyabonirsky whose research on 'The science of lasting happiness', concluded that while fifty percent of the determinants of happiness rests on inherited genes, ten percent depend on circumstances, and forty percent on intentional activity. This is quite revealing in the sense that mental and behavioral strategies adopted are quite important factors in determining happiness. Man can be master of this forty percent through training, self-conditioning and through determined action.

However, since fifty percent of what brings happiness is dependent on hereditary factors, this gives rise to questioning the validity of assertions that our actions alone can determine our future happiness. Presently we seem to have no control over this fifty percent of our hereditary make up, an important component in our self. But again recent scientific research after the discovery of the double-helix structure of the DNA that enabled the understanding of how genes control the chemical processes in a cell,[36] and the cracking of human genome[37] there is still hope that with genetic manipulations scientists may in future give greater scope for taking control of genetic determinants and ensuring greater happiness.

In the **Sukhi Parivaar or Happy Family** program a conscious effort is made by all members of the family to communicate regularly and share their daily experiences. When this is done with each one relating the day's moments of hardship or success, the members get knit into strong family ties, supporting and empathizing with one another, and feeling loved and united. By putting their heads together they are able to find solutions to their problems, and support one another in a spirit of solidarity. This leads to the greater happiness of all members by manipulating the forty percent mentioned in the earlier paragraphs. Here we are ourselves in control of our future happiness by consciously and collaboratively charting the future.

Many people take to evil ways with recourse to drugs, sex or alcohol to forget their problems. Happiness eludes them when they have no one to support them and share their miseries. Within a well knit family, such evils are minimized as they are surrounded by kiths and kins with whom they can emphasize and communicate. They can then get the support they need to get over their problems. Timely help and advice can change their lives.

> *'Happiness is inward, and not outward; and so, it does not depend on what we have, but on what we are.'*
>
> ***—Henry Van Dyke***

Chapter XVIII

Autonomous Development and Examples to Follow

Happiness requires that first of all basic needs have to be met. And the most important one is availability of food to satisfy our hunger and give us the energy to work. When food is scarce, people become restless, and open rebellion against the government starts. Food security is the first essential condition for a stable country. How then do we solve the problems of hunger in a world where the population is all the time increasing?

We have embraced a path where most people are trained to go for white collar jobs or to technical work and away from the soil. In the early days before the advent of modern education, a great proportion of the population was living in rural areas, tilling their fields and providing food for themselves and for those who could not produce the same. They were wise enough to save for the rainy day and for when calamities would strike. Leo Tolstoy[38] and Mahatma Gandhi[39] encouraged simple rural life where peace and harmony prevailed. However, industrialization and the search for better paying jobs took many out of the land to urban life, and agriculture had to move into the hands of large scale producers who could control the market. Few children took to agriculture as they preferred the gloss and glamour of urban life. When the elderly population was too weak to practice farming, dependence on others, especially the large scale producers, to grow food increased. And the market for agricultural products became a tool for social and political control.

Dependence on Others Even for Food

These days we have to rely on other people and countries that produce staple crops that we import and exchange for our industrial goods and services. Autonomy has decreased and we are at the whims of global players who control our lives. The good old principle of self dependence and producing extra for sharing with our neighbors has gone into the backyard. And our lifestyles have changed drastically! We are all the while rushing against time in static jobs, increasing our body weight and blood pressure. Children are becoming obese and disease prone with readily available junk food! Mothers have no time to cook a healthy dish for the family! And this is the price we pay for our so called civilization where physical and psychological diseases are on the increase!

Junk Food and Gyms

With food produced and marketed on large scale with all the attractive artificial additives, we have tendency to go for junk food. And when we have weight problems and become disease prone, we are advised to exercise, jog, go to gyms, practice meditation, and find happiness and peace within! **Gyms** are proliferating all around. Most hotels cater for them and even if you do not use them your bill has their value inbuilt. These days, in their efforts to please the young ones and win the votes of the population, governments are themselves building gyms in all places and encouraging a lifestyle that needs to be constantly reviewed.

Just see this irony of present lifestyle! The gentleman and lady clad in sporting suits and costly techie cushioned shoes are jogging along the tracks, often especially built for them, when just on the sides, the poor gardener is hoeing the field or planting the seeds, bent over and sweating profusely! He does not need a jogging session or costly membership at the gym club. He is simply being productive, working hard to produce food and flowers for others. And at night, the moment he throws himself on the bed, he is taken away into the world of restful sleep in the arms of Morpheus!

Kitchen Gardens

Common sense would have dictated that every house and every corner of cities have space for gardening and producing natural organic foods for the people. This will not only encourage people to undertake physical labor, exercise fruitfully and stay healthy and productive, but also produce food for themselves and for those who cannot do hard labor. Our health and hospital bills would reduce, our food importation would decrease, and governments would save millions that could be invested in more productive activities. And on top of that, we would enjoy fresh and healthy organic food!

There is now a growing consciousness on the need for physical labor, and even world famous personalities have started small kitchen gardens where they toil and sweat while producing healthy food for their kitchen.

Michelle Obama's Example

Michelle Obama,[40] the wife of President Barack Obama, has started an entire program on encouraging kitchen gardens with the participation of school children who learn how to grow fruits and vegetables, and avoid obesity and stay healthy. When the presidential couple moved into the White house, and their daughters Malia and Sasha two months later started gaining weight with so much eating out in parties and quick convenient fast food meals, Michelle started a program on kitchen gardening called 'Let's Move', along with Washington elementary school kids who had or were prone to similar obesity problems. She hopes to encourage the nation to start similar programs, and believes that such an activity could end obesity within a generation. Whenever VIP's visit the White House, the spouses invariably admire her small kitchen garden where she personally works and produces fine fruits and vegetables. They often get a jar of home made pickle as souvenir!

In cities the inhabitants are encouraged to use any available space, including abandoned lots and community spaces.

Michelle Obama Joins Kids to Harvest
the White House Garden

Autonomous Development

Autonomous development in a globalized world may look as an anachronism, but these days, with the advent of global warming and climate change, countries have already started feeling the pinch of devastation caused by natural calamities, and are not always ready to export food and other essential items so as to ensure their own survival. Priority is given to their own needs. This is where autonomous development has to be encouraged especially as concerns essential basic needs. This should not prevent those who produce excess goods to export them to countries that need them, in a spirit of fair trade.

As food production is reduced because of these calamities, food prices increase, and the poor are the first victims. In order to keep pace with the increase in prices of essential food items and essential commodities, and in order to enable the people to acquire the essentials, governments have to increase salaries and wages so as to contain mass uprising. This impacts on balance of payments and governments risk becoming heavily indebted. Had autonomous development been given the importance it deserves, such situations could have been avoided.

Hence there is a need to review our development policies, starting with our educational policies, and prepare the citizens to adopt an autonomous development path. Producing one's own food is the first step towards such a path.

Chapter XIX

Bringing Back Family Values

'There is only one thing more powerful than all the armies of the world. That is an idea whose time has come.'

—Victor Hugo

'Throughout my life I have always believed that the greatest gift in this world is not wealth, fame and power but the deep love of those you love.'

***—Edouard Lim Fat*[41]**

As the basic unit of society, the family is the place where concepts of human values are nurtured and implanted in the minds of people as from an early age. Human society that is made up of individual beings, cannot stay away from all that nature has provided, living and non-living. When members of a family go astray, their impact on society can be significant, and depending on the nature and intensity of the crime, the fall out does affect the living environment. Even before the individual in the society develops negative inclinations, it is necessary through the Sukhi Parivaar program to mould the character so that the negative forces outside the home will not win over the innate good that the person embodies.

Today, as families are becoming nuclear and individualism is becoming the norm, social problems abound and increase. One of the main reasons is that family values are not given the importance they deserve in our educational systems and the development paradigms adopted by economic growth conscious and obsessed policy makers. Unless family values are brought back and nurtured, we are heading for a self-destructing society. Many civilizations have come and disappeared in human history, sometimes because of the nature of human activity that were in dissonance with the physical and non-material environment.

The Need for Family Values

Our evolution started within family structures that fought for basic survival needs in the face of other invading species. Families grew into expanded social units, local communities and nations, and further into international organizations with objectives to promote mutual support, peace, harmony, cooperation and humane development. The multiple United Nations Organizations are the last in the series before we come up with inter-planetary and inter-galactic organizations as we evolve.

For these objectives to be universally achievable, it is necessary to start with the very first unit, the family, and strengthen it with values that can sustain mankind. The basic values are the same, reflecting inter-personal relations, and form the core of our aspirations for a happy and progressive society. We will now see what these family values are and ways to bring them back in our fold.

Parental Care and Obligations

When children are born in a family (something that is becoming rarer in 'developed' societies where selfish individualism is glorified!), the parents care for them until they can stand on their own legs. Parents often go through a lot of sacrifice to ensure that the children do not suffer in later life and are able to grow into great people contributing to global advancement. At one time, parental care of the children was a must because parents needed the same children to support them in their old age. Such care and support are being gradually taken over by the state that has to rely more and more on carers and new technologies and robots to assist in doing the same. While physical needs are being partly met, the emotional needs are becoming rarer.

At the same time, because of child abuse by some parents, children's rights have been proclaimed by the United Nations and some governments. This forces the parents to care for their children, failing which they run the risk of prosecution. In some quarters children have become so aware of their rights that they threaten parents and even inform the authorities on any minor abuse. In many societies, 'Spare the rod and spoil the child' is now a relic of another generation! We have to reeducate the parents on their parental duties, highlighting the need for constant interaction and dialogue with their children to keep the relationships alive.

As children grow and start asserting themselves, the attitude and attention of parents to them need to change. As soon as the signs of adolescence start showing, parents should consider the children more as friends and get to know their sentiments. They should encourage the children to confide in them, and then guide them accordingly. Winning such confidence and trust is not always easy. Parents, through their sacrifice, should highlight their concern for the welfare of the adolescents and help them accordingly.

When the children become grown-ups and have their own family, parents should, as far as possible, try not to interfere in their daily problems, unless the children ask for their support. The proverbial son-in-law, mother-in-law strained relationships or the daughter-in-law mother-in-law relationships have to be carefully watched.

Filial Obligations

The duties of children towards their parents are being fast forgotten. Grown up children prefer to move or stay away from parents with whom their bonds are no more as strong as when they were small. When they get married, their wife has a say on their independence, especially when both partners are working. In 'developed' societies old parents are left to themselves, ending up in homes where they miss the love of their children. If they get a telephone call from them once in a way, it's a special treat! And if they take the trouble of visiting them, it's a big event in the lives of these old people.

Grown up children should be made aware of the fact that with age the parents become more and more emotional and wish to share the moments with their children and grand-children. There is nothing worse than seeing old parents sighing in front of family albums, and hoping the family were together in moments of joy and sorrow. The will to live for another day reduces in spite of all the material comforts and amenities available, and in spite of the government assisting them by different means.

Missing the love of the family is a curse of the modern generation! Parents crave for the presence of grand children in their midst. They could forget most of their daily problems, aches and ailments, if the grand children were around. But the pattern of modern industrial and technological development has deprived old parents of this primary need. Information technology has sometimes brought them together for short moments, but the warmth of proximity, the soft touch of the children's hands, are missing. We often wonder whether the new generation is aware of this need.

In many cases the pressures of work or economic stringencies keep the working children unwilling to get married and have children of their own. Some see the birth of children as obstacles and liabilities to their professional pursuits, not realizing that some day their turn will come when they will face the same situation as their old parents. Hence there is urgent need to bring back the family bond that can be the main source of emotional and material support for the elderly. The Sukhi Parivaar program, through its stress on constant dialogue within the family when the children are still young, can develop the necessary understanding and bonds that can keep families united in all times.

Fraternal Relations

As young siblings children are attached to one another, and as they grow up, instead of strengthening, the bonds loosen. In many cases this is due to the pressure of the working environment, the craze for greater material comforts, competition for family resources and the development of selfishness. Most of the family feuds start with some brother or sister trying to grab or be unjust in the sharing of family wealth. This inability to share properly is the result of years of living together when the seeds of mutual understanding, compassion and the spirit of sharing were not adequately inculcated by the parents and the teachers.

We often hear of brothers resorting to violence when their desires are not fulfilled. History is replete with wars between brothers to rule the kingdoms. But there are rare cases where, as in the Indian epic Ramayana, the younger brother preferred to keep away from the throne that rightly belonged to the elder brother, sacrificing himself of the luxuries of kingship, as a mark of fraternal love and respect. Such fraternal relationships are indeed very rare now, as modern development has greatly killed such values.

The love and attachment between brothers and sisters have, in some societies, been preserved by religious and cultural practices, like the Indian festival of 'Rakhi' when the sister ties a thread to the brother's wrist as an emblem of her love and his promise to protect her in all adversities. But such practice is becoming rarer, and in western societies, it is completely absent. Through the Sukhi Parivaar program such values can be brought back.

Father's and Mother's Day

Through globalization and the impact of the world media, more and more countries are now celebrating father's and mother's day every year as a day devoted to the love and recognition of parents. Children, young and old, are reminded of their duty towards their parents. Those living in the vicinity of the parents visit them with gifts, and those far away make a point to call them and wish them health and long life.

While in some societies the celebration of one day annually in the name of the father or mother is considered an aberration, for every day should be considered as a day to please parents, in others this is a cultural tradition. It is often exploited for commercial ends and for show business. Presenting costly gifts to parents once in the year can never replace their longing for constant love and affection. The real filial love and affection could be missing. Perhaps this could be remedied through the Sukhi Parivaar program by educating children on the need for constant attention to parents, especially when they are growing old.

Respect for the Elderly

Grandparents had a great role in pre-industrial societies when the care of the grandchildren was their responsibility when parents were busy in their work. After retirement the elderly had something interesting to keep them busy and healthy. Accompanying the kids to school and then bringing them back, playing with them and looking after their welfare were part of their activities. This has diminished or disappeared these days, except in some rare rural communities, joint families or traditional societies. Grandparents were the persons who used to tell stories of heroes and impart a sense of values in children. We are leaving this to kindergartens where unfortunately, very often impersonal relationships develop. Grandparents, living far from them, are often left in 'homes' to spend the rest of their lives. This is the price of modern 'civilization'!

Neither do the children benefit from the love and attention of grandparents, nor do the elderly enjoy the respect, love and company of the grandchildren. In the process family bonds weaken and individualism becomes pronounced. By keeping the grandparents with the family, we not only enrich their lives, but also ensure that family values are not forgotten. Sukhi

Parivaar draws the attention of the people on the need to integrate the elderly and bring back the family values.

Encouraging Friendly Relations

Besides normal parent-child relationships, the members in a family need to develop friendly relationships so that communication becomes more open-hearted and trust develops. Communications between parent and children, brothers and sisters, husband and wife, often lack the openness that can strengthen the bonds. Why should children speak their hearts to friends outside and not open up to parents? Unless parents make an effort to behave like friends with their kids, they will not be able to understand them properly, and thus not be able to offer the necessary solutions to problems based on their own experience. Parents, besides doing their normal parental duty, must play with the kids, at times behave like them to drive home certain truths, and then only they can better grasp the feelings of the young ones.

Similar friendly relationships should be developed between husband and wife; then only mutual love and understanding can be sustained through thick and thin. Children are good observers, and when they note the strained relationship between parents, they are the first to be psychologically affected. This then affects their own behavior. If they have lived amidst loving parents who shared everything like good friends, their attitude to life and ability to face difficulties are such as to make of them exemplary citizens.

Regular Get-Togethers

When members of a family are in the vicinity, every effort must be made to get the family members together as often as possible. All occasions like birthdays, marriages, deaths, cultural festivals, picnics and outings, celebrations of special events, offer opportunities to get family members together, share a family prayer, some food and drink, and most of all, share the moments together. Some close knit families make it a point to meet for every Sunday lunch or dinner, and avail of the opportunity to share their joys, sorrows, and problems. This strengthens their mutual trust and solidarity.

As for members who live in the same house, parents and children, the program encourages daily get-togethers before dinners, as in family communions. Such communions have the power to strengthen bonds and create peace and harmony in the family, along with the multiple benefits mentioned earlier.

These family values need either to be brought back or strengthened so as to have a happy family, a happy society and a happy world. Such values affect both mind and the heart, the intellect and the emotion, and both have to be nurtured, consciously catered for in order to develop a healthy, happy environment in a sustainable world where harmony, peace, sharing, solidarity and mutual love endure. This is what we hope for the future, a legacy we can leave for future generations, and it is within our capacity to realize it. It starts with our efforts within our own family and the blessings of the Almighty.

And to realize it all partners in the family have to act together.

Possibility of Fostering Wrong Family Values

In the early years of a child's development, the family environment has a very great influence in shaping the child's future. Invariably the future is marked by imprints in the child's memory during these formative years. Children often tend to copy the parents. To gain the parents' attention and love the children please them by yielding to their demands. In the process distinctive character traits are imbibed. As the years go by, the three elements that continue marking the development are the inherited characteristics, the parental influence, and the society's influence, with varying degrees.

Where parents consciously try to develop certain religious self-sacrificial traits that border on intolerance and rebellion, the result is the growth of suicide bombers, jihadis, and terrorists. This is where parents need to be educated by the authorities as a priority. The needs of the parents in terms of food, shelter, clothing, education, health and employment are prerequisites and have to be met by all means, often with international collaboration.

While we are keen to ensure that universal family values are kept alive and transmitted from generation to generation, we must also be aware that in some societies, especially conservative ones where feudal traditions are maintained even now, we run the risk of perpetuating such traditions through the Sukhi Parivaar exercise. It is normal for parents in such societies to pass on the traditions to their children with the hope that they will also enjoy the benefits of the feudal traditions. This cannot be allowed in a modern society, and thus there is need for monitoring at the micro level to ensure that no negative traditions or destructive values are being promoted by parents. This can happen in tribal areas where family feuds are common, or in extremist religious groups where suicide bombers or guerilla warfare are still present.

In all societies there are some traditions that can have negative impacts on society at large, and such traditions cannot be entertained in the name of family values. Such traditions tend to perpetuate inequities, social discriminations, divisions within the communities based on birth privileges, autocracy and other evils. The Sukhi Parivaar program cannot entertain such traditions in the name of family values. On the other hand it tries to promote such universal values as are inherent in the declarations and resolutions of the United Nations Organization where peoples of different origins struggle to reach consensus on issues affecting mankind.

Can the program apply to households where parents are alcoholics and fighting all the time, where basic needs are not met, and where the family spirit has little meaning? In slums and poverty-torn areas where the daily struggle for survival is an ever demanding task? The success of the program naturally rests on the ability of parents to join hands and work for the benefit of the family. The education of parents by socio-cultural and religious organizations as well as by the local governments that cater for their basic needs then becomes a prerequisite. Otherwise children in such families would follow the paths shown by the parents, and 'sukhi parivaar' would be a vain program!

No Brave New World, Please!

Family traditions differ in different societies, but the essential family values are universal and eternal. It is such values that can sustain humanity, away from the concept of Aldous Huxley's 'Brave New World'[42] where technology can create new species that are devoid of the presence of essential feelings that enrich mankind. Our present trends, with the pronounced inclination towards a materialist civilization, have already started showing the cracks and a gradual demise of family values. It is hence necessary for humanity to preserve what is left and bring back what has been lost in terms of family values, if we do not want to destroy ourselves through selfish individualism, greed, ruthless competition, mistrust and exploitation of one another.

We can never go back in time. But those values that have been lost through a misguided development path can be brought back. The advent of new science and technology with its evolved tools of communication can help us to expedite a new education based on eternal family values.

I pray that the Brave New World will never come! Human beings who have the blessings of the Creator who endowed them with feelings, have to survive and not become heartless robots. Instead, we need a world where happiness can prevail, where joys, laughter, sadness are what life is made of, and where Sukhi Parivaar through family communion can play its unique role.

What Future? The Living Earth Simulator

Scientific research on ways and means to bring greater happiness and improve the lot of mankind is enhancing man's horizon and capacity, and is an ongoing process. With the development of more and more powerful computers, scientists are coming up with new models for our development that incorporates both social and hard sciences. Multidisciplinary research is the order of the day. The hard sciences have led us to greater individual material welfare, but social problems are on the rise, and happiness keeps eluding us!

At the Swiss Federal Institute of Technology,[43] Dr. Helbing who holds the Chair of the Future ICT Project, has gathered an international group of researchers who are trying to develop a simulator that can measure the state of the society that would account for major factors like health, education and environment. '*And last but not least, happiness*', says Dr. Helbing. "Many problems we have today - including social and economic instabilities, wars, disease spreading - are related to human behavior, but there is apparently a serious lack of understanding regarding how society and the economy work," says Dr Helbing.

We hope this research with the development of a 'knowledge accelerator' similar to the Great Hadron Collider of fundamental particles at CERN[44] which is trying to understand our physical environment, will lead to a greater understanding of both the physical and social environment, with our struggle for happiness, and hence contribute to it.

Meanwhile, the Sukhi Parivaar program, on the other hand, is more down to earth, more practical, more basic, and achievable by all good-willed citizens working for a better world, and starting with their own families. Their families are primarily their responsibilities much more than the responsibilities of their governments and the organizations working to improve their lot.

Hence the urgent need to adopt the program and bring universal family values back through family communion!

Epilogue

These days the world is going through turmoil with unexpected events in numerous parts of the globe. With globalization and the power of the media, people are becoming conscious of their rights and privileges, and are sometimes being educated as to their duties as well. A new philosophy of life and of development is felt, with developed economies facing economic woes, social disruptions and environmental catastrophes. At the same time, powers that for generations had ruled, many with a semblance of democracy or with outright dictatorship are being questioned and often just thrown out through rebellions, like in North Africa.

In many developed countries where material wealth has turned people into extreme consumerist individualists and where family ties and values are fast disappearing, disenchanted people are resorting to either violence or to the search for spiritual fulfillment. The ravages of global warming and climate change, of greed and global financial crisis, and of repression by violent means are forcing people to rethink about their existence on a resource constrained earth and in this vast universe. While one part of the globe has witnessed rapid wealth creation, other parts have been reduced to growing impoverishment and different forms of violence have taken roots. Peaceful coexistence is threatened, and remedial measures to contain violence are proving ineffective. The right mix of material and spiritual development is of crying necessity. And proper education is the way ahead.

In such a context, the preventive measures as suggested in the text, where the powers of family communion have been highlighted, can make a significant change. There is nothing new about having regular family dialogues, but the way we do the same and the spirit behind such dialogues have to be understood and brought into action. The complex psycho-sociological factors that affect our thoughts and actions have to be further researched and understood. Scientific discoveries are bringing new insights as we go along, and if we keep our minds open to 'progressive' views, as against medieval ego-centrist prescriptions, we are likely to make quantum jumps in our development paradigms. We have seen how greed-based pseudo-sciences have brought about global catastrophes on the physical, social and environmental planes of our existence.

The views expressed are far from being prescriptive,[45] but are suggestions for enabling a new future for all of us. A future based on mutual trust arising from open heart to heart dialogue between partners in the primary cell of society, the family. If all of us could take care of our family by responsibly assuming our primary roles as properly educated parents eager to bring happiness within the fold, the situation will definitely change. That is why such dialogues need to bring under consideration our own lives as members of a much greater human family, and not ignore what is happening amidst our neighbors and in other countries of our planet. The marvels of modern media communication are slowly reaching all homes, and we have no excuse for closing our own doors to the positive impacts that they can bring, while remembering that like most technologies, we have to differentiate the grain from the chaff.

The Sukhi Parivaar program[46] offers a ray of hope in this mad race to global development, emphasizing the urgent need to bring greater spiritual understanding in the material welfare of people. If only we can realize that our welfare is closely linked with all beings, our kiths and kins, as well as the entire human race and the other species that inhabit our biosphere, our vision will change and happiness can be nearer.

The future is in our own hands!

Where dreams are allowed

Where dreams are allowed to become reality,
And love, not greed is the primal force of life,
Where one takes delight in what one does
And gives one's all to fulfill it,
Where day by day, joy accumulates and sorrow wanes,
And the bird sings the birth of a new bright dawn,
While nature breathes a new breath of life,

Where Presidents and Ministers weep for the good
Of those who put their trust in them,
And where parents and teachers
Crave for devoted children
And are prepared to give their life for them,
Without shirking their divine responsibility,

Where the mind soars into the infinity of space and time,
And finds its energy for tirelessly moving forward,
Into that realm, Oh Lord, let my planet move!

Mahatma Gandhi Memorial Lecture'Mahatma Gandhi's Philosophy and Its Relevance Today'

Proclaiming a New Philosophy of Life

Moka, 4th October 2010.

It is an honour for me to deliver this Memorial Lecture to mark the birth of Mahatma Gandhi, the world known political and spiritual leader, born on 2nd October1869. At the very outset, may I thank the Mahatma Gandhi Institute for inviting me to deliver this talk. The topic of this lecture is: 'Mahatma Gandhi's philosophy and its relevance today.'

When we look around us and see war and violence in different forms as an everyday occurrence, when we see what is happening in the home country of Mahatma Gandhi, we start wondering whether the Mahatma's philosophy has any relevance today. A civilization based on unfair competition and aggressive capitalism has taken over, and people are being lured by it. But when we also see the most pressing present global problems, we realize that we still need another Gandhi, or that at least we need to abide by his teachings.

Since there are many young people here, I wish to relate my own initiation to Gandhism. I was eight years old when the Mahatma died, and the moment the news reached us on 30th January 1948, my father came rushing home from his work to announce this. As a kid I was playing at the foot of a big coconut tree in our yard. It must have been around 4 p.m. Immediately my father told us all to start fasting. No food in the evening, and to me it was an experience. We rushed to the home of the richest man Babuji Ramdour in the village of Bon Accueil where I lived, the only house in the vicinity that had a radio, a big cabinet type box placed in the verandah as a show case. People were flocking from all around. Mahatma Gandhi's favorite song was on: *'Raghupati Raaghava Raaja Raam, Patita paawan Sitaa Raam. Ishwar Allah tere naam, sabhko sanmati de Bhagavan!'* Everybody was mourning. Since then on, the impression of Gandhi stayed in my mind. I am saying this because it is necessary that we introduce Gandhi to our children from a very early age. Gandhi's book, 'My experiments with truth', should be read by every young adolescent, and if this memorial lecture can have an impact, I invite our policy makers to ensure that this text be prescribed as a text book or reading book for our schools. I myself read it while an adolescent in my secondary school.

How about his philosophy and its relevance? I will start by highlighting the global events that are affecting mankind today, and show how by not following the philosophy of Mahatma Gandhi, we are destroying our beautiful blue-green planet and all that is in it. Our future looks grim, but there is hope since, forced by global catastrophes, a gradual awakening is taking place both amidst the common masses and the decision makers. So let us not despair! I will not repeat myself with recall of his life and achievements, that most of you already know, but will restrict myself to showing the relevance of his teachings, and end by quoting a few of his philosophical statements and show how they are as relevant as ever for the salvation of mankind.

Global Warming and Climate Change

Let us start with what we are witnessing today: Global warming and climate change with consequent suffering of mankind, as well as the global financial crisis that is leading millions to unemployment.

Our present civilization, with all the gloss and glamour of a technological age, has erred by adopting a development paradigm[47] based on unsustainable exploitation of natural resources and by believing in a materialist path that has as objective to increase human welfare by mainly increasing the world's Gross Domestic Product (GDP). Some leaders influenced by the capitalist model, profess that by such a growth, there will be a trickle-down effect and everybody will benefit by a higher standard of living. Many western countries and a few in the East have also espoused this philosophy, and indeed there has been an increase in the world's GDP, with some increase in the standard of living, but a decrease in quality of life and the trickle-down effect has yet to materialize![48] The disparity between the rich and the poor has grown, and while some are wallowing in wealth, others are suffering from a dire want of basic needs.

What is this phenomenon of global warming? Our planet has witnessed a very slow increase in its temperature during millenniums, but a very rapid increase within the last three hundred years since the advent of the industrial revolution. This, as the effect of man's lifestyles bearing on a growing consumption of the non-renewable natural resources and destruction of biodiversity. We have taken much more from nature and replaced it by energy intensive concrete-based infrastructures that are not self-sustaining. We have used increasing amounts of fossil fuels that had taken millions of years to form. And the rate of this consumption has accelerated during these last few decades. In the early days we used to have energy based on biomass like wood and replaced the biomass by planting more or allowing nature to regenerate itself. But of late our 'civilized beings' are just consuming whatever is left of this biomass and not replacing it by new plantations, exploiting the non-renewable fossil fuels for multiple usages: industry, transport, cooking, washing, heating, cooling, and you name it! It has now transpired that globally we consume so much of the fossil fuels that burning them has released excess toxic substances that are harming the environment. Can you believe that daily we are releasing **eighty million tons of CO_2** in the atmosphere, and this is growing every year?[49]

The release of this CO_2 into the atmosphere is producing a **greenhouse effect** that is increasing the temperature of the atmosphere. It's like when we are in a room with closed glass windows receiving the hot sunshine. Our world is like having a fever that is growing daily, and this is causing damage to the environment and leading to climate change. Our summers and winters are changing in intensity, and the new weather patterns are bringing about the birth of new forms of bacteria and viruses. Did our ancestors hear of Chikungunya, AN1H1, Mad-cow disease, AIDS and the like? Every year new diseases are plaguing our populations! The new weather patterns are also producing more severe rainfalls and floods with millions losing their lives and belongings, forest fires and droughts destroying crops and property, and leading to rise in commodity prices. The poor are the most hit. Who is responsible for all this? It's not Nature but we, human beings, by our greed and lifestyles! You will now ask me what has this to do with Mahatma Gandhi's philosophy. Do you remember what **Mahatma Gandhi had said. 'There is enough for everybody's need on this planet, but not enough for everyone's greed.'** If only we had understood the implications of his visionary statement, and acted accordingly! It is man's greed that has led to the global catastrophes we now witness. Starting from the East to the West, climatic changes are affecting people by the millions. Forest fires in US California, Russia, China, Australia, tropical storms, cyclones, typhoons in Caribbean countries, southern US, Bay of Bengal, China, India, floods in China, India, England, France and Nigeria, all these because we did not follow the philosophy and lifestyle proposed by Mahatma Gandhi, the visionary!

We espoused an economic development paradigm based on the concept of **'Economies of scale',** proposed by big profit-motivated economists like Adam Smith[50] and the like, and accepted mass manufacture of goods like cars and vehicles following the American manufacturer Ford, and in the process gobbling more and more of energy in the form of fossil fuels. We accepted centralization of production units concentrated around urban areas, leading to mass movement of rural populations seeking employment opportunities and better livelihoods. In the process we destroyed family structures that had for generations depended on mutual solidarity, love and sharing, simple way of living in harmony with nature. The joint family system died a slow death, and if still present in some cultures, is fast dying now. Is this what Gandhi had proposed? Is this what we want?

As opposed to this concentration of industries, Mahatma Gandhi who, during his student days in

England, had witnessed the squalor of the factory workers in the textile mills of Manchester, wanted the Graam Udyog system, with decentralization of industries, and the spread of cottage small-scale industries all over the country. Such industries utilize locally produced renewable energy through solar, wind, water and biomass, causing less release of CO_2 and other toxic gasses. Hence hardly any global warming! Some farsighted economists like **John Galbraith and Ernst Frederic Schumacher** understood this and promoted this concept. They were admirers of Mahatma Gandhi. Schumacher[51] even wrote a book entitled 'Small is Beautiful'. For those interested in global development, this is a must-read book. But the accepted development paradigm based on the concept of 'mass manufacture and economies of scale' has persisted up to now. Hopefully, with the realization of the havoc of global warming, this can change, provided each and every one of us accept to reduce our consumption patterns and adopt a simpler, less energy intensive lifestyle, based on Gandhi's philosophy of frugality. Unfortunately, at the universities worldwide, Adam Smith's theories are still studied with utmost seriousness by our budding economists!

Global Financial Crisis

Linked with this type of development based on greed, wastage and unfair competition is the advent of the present global financial crisis. The world is presently going through a prolonged period of reduced economic growth, the outcome of a financial crisis triggered by greedy bankers and insurance brokers involved in liberally giving loans to home buyers. When the home owners could not pay back, the banks had to declare bankruptcy. This financial crisis has led to massive retrenchment of workers, increased unemployment, and misery to millions of bread-earners and their families. To keep certain industries and enterprises running and avoid further retrenchment, some governments have had to dole out generous stimulus packages to owners whose profit margins had decreased drastically, and who were not prepared to sacrifice their own personal lifestyles. In the United States some of them shamelessly used their private jet-planes to reach Washington with a begging bowl! The dearth of money on the global financial market has forced many governments to reduce their normal spending on meeting basic needs of their populations. Health, social aid and education programs have to bear the crunch and the poor and the needy are the most affected. Do we realize the miseries of those millions that are losing their jobs as factories are closing down, and industrial activities are on the wane? If there is increased social tension, strife and violence, if crimes are increasing all around and people are resorting to drugs and alcohol to forget their miseries, on whom shall we put the blame? Had we followed Mahatma Gandhi's philosophy of living in harmony with nature, with thriftiness and frugality in our consuming what we have received from nature, would this have happened?

Harmony in Thought, Word and Deed

Mahatma Gandhi taught us to harmonize our thoughts, words and actions, to be integral human beings devoid of hypocrisy. He never preached something that he did not practice himself. As an illustration, when he returned from South Africa to India in 1915 and saw the plight of the small planters in the rural areas, he decided to live in their midst and fight for their rights. Chronic unemployment and underemployment affected the peasants, and their sufferance and poverty led him to start his Sarvodaya[52] and Gram Udyog[53] movements from Sewagram or Segaon. He led a simple village life in a hut with minimal amenities, dressed like them, and worked with the people and for them, educating them and awakening their consciousness on their duties and rights. Village industries started there and spread in many areas of India. But the slowness of the impact of his rural development activity did not impress the western educated bureaucrats at the top who preferred the western model of fast economic development. Had such village industries backed by his promotion of 'Basic education schools' taken root and spread, today we would not have had the majority of the population in India still living in neglected rural areas and in poverty. Let us remember what Gandhi said: *'Good travels at a snail's pace...'* To express his sentiments on being authentic, he said: *'Always aim at complete harmony of thought and word and deed. Always aim at purifying your thoughts and everything will be well.'* On another occasion he said: *'Happiness is when what you think, what you say, and what you do are in harmony.'* Alas, very few practice this philosophy! We learn to be diplomatic in order to succeed, an ephemeral success indeed! For in the end, and deep within, our conscience tortures us, unless by repeated similar acts we have killed this conscience within us. Temporary and ephemeral success can never bring lasting happiness.

A Paragon of Humility

Gandhi taught us to be humble as we are all humans, liable to make mistakes, and to accept our mistakes and be ready to change. He said: *'I claim to be a simple individual liable to err like any other mortal. I own, however, that I have humility enough to confess my errors and to retrace my steps.'* Few people portray such humility, and often claim to be righteous in their actions. If only they could learn from Gandhi's philosophy, the world would be a different place.

Self-Sufficiency as a Way of Life, a Way of Economic Development

Mahatma Gandhi promoted the philosophy of self-sufficiency in his Sarvodaya program. He wanted each town or village to be self-sufficient in terms of food, energy, water and other basic needs, including employment. This concept did not capture the minds and interest of profit-motivated entrepreneurs who believed in 'economies of scale' and mass production for export. They preferred to exploit cheap labor and produce for exporting to other regions, thereby increasing their profits. Gandhi on the other hand said that one should export only whatever is in excess after local consumption. He had seen how farmers were exploited by the colonial masters and the 'zamindars'. This is what led him to adopting 'swadeshi' goods like the khadi cloth that could be produced at village level, and that provided employment to the people.

Now that global financial crisis and recession have shown their tentacles, a new philosophy is coming in. Unemployment within developed economies increased when countries, hoping to maximize profits, resorted to outsourcing of expertise, labor and manufacturing. Now companies are going back home to restart their activities because of lack of money available on the international market. Banks have become more cautious in their lending. So we are going back to the philosophy of self-sufficiency. Greed has shown its disastrous impacts.

Here in Mauritius it was strongly believed that the sugar industry should have priority support, thereby killing small producers of milk and milk products, fruits, pulses and vegetables. Now wisdom is dawning back on the policy-makers who realize that self-sufficiency in food is a priority. We cannot rely on external producers who are being harassed by the vagaries of climate change that is causing food prices to rise constantly. And we are now struggling with a budget deficit. So once again we see the relevance of Gandhi's philosophy of self-sufficiency.

Globalization and interdependency are ideals we have to work for, but we must ensure that local needs are met as a priority. The philosophy of self-sufficiency can ensure that external forces will not exploit the masses, and that people take control of their own lives. Too often we let others control our lives when we have the powers within to take care of it. Through empowerment we rouse these powers for our own development.

Empowerment and Service to the Poor

Empowering the masses is the greatest human achievement we can envisage. History has shown that civilizations based on exploitation of the weak have always failed. Gandhi's philosophy of service to the poor and the suffering masses in a spirit of love, mutual trust and sharing of resources is back on the global scene. International organizations and NGO's are stressing on the need to empower the people. Mahatma Gandhi promoted it through his 'sarvodaya' program. He is known to have said: '*Man becomes great exactly in the degree in which he works for the welfare of his fellow-men.*'

Our world still needs people like him, for there are millions still groping for a morsel of food, millions still with no potable drinking water and basic health facilities, no proper schooling, and no sense of self-respect. In spite of the efforts of the United Nations Organization, much remains to be done. Gandhi had realized that the service of the people is easier when we understand that all humanity is one, and that the same Supreme Spirit resides in all of us. This led him to love all irrespective of their caste, creed or colour. In Africa he served all, including the blacks, and in India, his struggle to empower the Harijans opened the door for integration. He did not believe in social barriers created by man against man, and in every one of his actions the spirit of service was uppermost.

Another one of his famous statements reads as follows: '*Whenever you are in doubt, or when the self becomes too much with you, apply the following test. Recall the face of the poorest and weakest man who you may have seen, and ask yourself if the step you contemplate is going to be of any use to him. Will he gain anything by it? Will it restore him to a control over his own life and destiny? In other words, will it lead to swaraj for the hungry and the starving millions? Then you will find your doubts and your self melt away.*' These appear in one of his last notes written in 1948 just before he was assassinated by a shortsighted fanatic.

If only this statement could be imbibed and followed to the word by each and every one of us, every action of ours would be viewed in a new light of love and service, and the world would grow into a better place for all. The inherent philosophy in this statement is today as relevant as ever and it is our duty to propagate it and practice it. We have to remind ourselves every now and then of the spirit therein, and strive to go by it. Our schools should teach children to recite it as a daily prayer, and world leaders should invoke it at the beginning of their deliberations. Then only our conscience will awaken and fructify into goodness for all.

As a last message from him, this statement embodies the fruits of his lifetime of struggle for and service to the poor and the forlorn. Hence the very basis of Gandhian philosophy. Its validity is felt all the more in the face of the multiple tragedies we witness daily: organized terrorism, crime and ruthless violence, wars and rebellions, repression and military dictatorship. He had a strong faith in the goodness of humanity, and never despaired even if the immediate results of his work were not as fruitful as he expected. And once he said: '*You must not lose faith in humanity. Humanity is like an ocean; if a few drops of the ocean are dirty, the ocean does not become dirty.*'

Non-Violence and Satyagraha

These lead us to another of his prominent beliefs and actions that have already contributed to change the world appreciably. That is his philosophy of Non-violence and Satyagraha or Soul-Force. He first experimented with it in South Africa on 7th June 1893, where, as a young barrister traveling in a first class compartment normally reserved for whites, he was thrown out, bag and baggage, on to the railway platform in Pietermaritzsburg. He refused to obey the policeman who, because of the Apartheid regime, could not allow him, in spite of his having a first class ticket, to stay in the carriage. Gandhi allowed himself to be bodily lifted and thrown out. He did not retaliate with violence, but coolly bore the blows and the insult. This behavior stemmed from his conviction in the rectitude of his action, and his faith in the eventual victory of right over wrong. He preferred physical sufferance to cowardice, and would not yield to brutality as long as his conviction dictated that what he was doing was the right thing. His spirit was indomitable and he believed in forgiving his oppressor. He has often said that Satyagraha is not the path of the weak but of the strong. It's the spiritual strength within, the Soul-Force, that enables people to follow Satyagraha as a means to oppose injustice and repression. As a practical idealist, he said: '*The religion of non-violence is not meant merely for the Rishis and the Saints. It is meant for the common people as well. Non-violence is the law of our species, as violence is the law of the brute. In its dynamic condition, it means conscious suffering. It does not mean meek submission to the will of the evil-doer, but it means the putting of one's whole soul against the will of the tyrant.*'

The four hundred kilometers Dandi Salt-March in 1930 was another occasion when Satyagraha proved to be a worthy weapon against repression. Hundreds and thousands of people were attracted by this strategy of ahimsa or non-violence. They were beaten up by the policemen, but did not retaliate. This roused the English against their own oppression. When he eventually succeeded in liberating India from British rule, other leaders followed suit. Nelson Mandela and Desmond Tutu in South Africa, Martin Luther King Jr in the United States, Dalai Lama in Tibet, and Aung San Su Kyi in Burma, adopted the same strategy. Gandhi said that this is not the strategy of the weak but that of the strong, strong in soul-force, strong in mind and spirit. Who would have ever thought that in the most powerful country of the world, where the sons and daughters of past slaves are in minority, a son of theirs, Barak Obama, would one day be elected democratically as the President of the United States of America? This is the end result of the Satyagraha once practiced by his predecessor, Martin Luther King

Jr. No wonder the United Nations has recognized the validity of his philosophy, and declared his birthday on every 2nd October as the International Day of Non-Violence.

The question now is whether this strategy is still valid in the face of terrorism and guerilla warfare. Can America adopt the same method in the war in Irak or Afghanistan? Can India adopt the same Gandhian principle in subjugating the cross-border terrorists in Kashmir? Can Aung San Su Kyi succeed in Burma without pressure from the West? It is difficult to say yes categorically. But one thing is for sure. If time is no constraint, non-violent methods will surely succeed.

For this to succeed, certain **prerequisites** have to be met. We must understand why people become terrorists, and empathize with them by meeting their basic needs first. A just sharing and distribution of local resources, provision of adequate opportunities for work and livelihood, respect for cultural differences, education for empowerment, these are among the prerequisites. Patience and a strong faith in the human goodness are essential. This is what Gandhi would have proposed if he were still alive. He used to say that we cannot fight evil with evil. *'An eye for an eye will make the whole world blind!'* One should fight evil and not the evil-doer. One has to isolate evil from the evil-doer, and destroy this evil with peaceful means, appealing to the spirit of the person. Hence the urgent need for forgiving the bad deeds of others and winning over their minds and hearts through conscious love and practical solidarity. Passive love cannot have the necessary impacts. Love has to be expressed through action, through service. The philosophy of non-violence is thus still valid, for it is based on positive values.

Present day western thought is based on the concept of 'Might is right', and 'Survival of the fittest'. This unfortunately is not able to achieve global peace, in spite of the thousands of United Nations resolutions, and the billions of dollars wasted in trying to maintain superficial peace, whether it is in Kashmir, Kosovo, Western Sahrawi, Congo, Darfur, Afghanistan and so many other places. There is need for greater promotion of the Non-Violence movement.

The Means to an End

Gandhi always emphasized the fact that the end does not justify the means. The process[54] is more important, and one should pay special attention to the nature of the process than on the end itself. This process has to be based on right thinking and right action, and if the process is devious, even a successful end will not be justified. Gandhi did not approve of the saying: All is fair in love and war! Crooked and unethical means are often resorted to just for the sake of achieving an end. Such an end may be appealing in the immediate future, but in the long run the end invariably brings failure and suffering.

It is said that righteous intention followed by righteous act will always bring peace and happiness. It is the righteous intention that counts most.

The Seven Social Sins

Mahatma Gandhi's philosophy is also **epitomized** in what he enumerated as the seven social sins. These are:

1. Politics without principles.
2. Wealth without work.
3. Pleasure without conscience.

4. Knowledge without character.
5. Commerce without morality.
6. Science without humanity.
7. Worship without sacrifice.

Politics without Principles

Let us take each of them and analyze them. Politics is often discredited by some as the 'last resort of scoundrels'. This is not always true, and may apply to some politicians, but not to all. We must remember that Christ, Mohammed and others were also politicians par excellence. Gandhi himself has been an exemplary politician who once headed the Indian National Congress. Yet these politicians, through their selfless actions, have changed the world to a very great extent. None of them grabbed power by unethical means, and amassed wealth for their progeny, and all they ever acquired were invested in the service of the people.

When politics is devoid of principles, it gives way to corruption and abuse of power. The principles necessary for righteous politics stand on the bedrock of truth, love, compassion and service to all. The moment we restrict our activities to a select few and ignore the common humanity we all share, we get bogged into the trap of self-delusion and short-sighted politics without principles. Gandhi's warning should be our guiding beacon. The world badly needs this, and Gandhi's philosophy should guide us all. For Gandhi, politics, religion, moral life and economic progress, culture, law and spirituality are all interwoven into a holistic development that can sustain not only humanity but all that our globe contains, the living and the non-living. Holistic development is not the same as a techno-industrial development that so many desire.

Wealth without Work

We often see people acquiring wealth through inheritance, or without having worked for it. Invariably such wealth is wasted and only physical structures, buildings without spirit, memories of debauchery survive. I have seen people sitting at their desk, clicking their computer mouse and transferring millions of dollars from one account to another in a split second and reaping windfall gains. You will say they are working with their brain. Good, but when no proper use is made of it, such people do not deserve our respect and admiration. God's gift of a powerful brain is meant for good work. When wealth is acquired without work, its value is not appreciated, and the tendency to abuse and waste is high.

India has the record number of billionaires, 69 as the latest global figure, and yet India also has one of the greatest number of poor living below the poverty line. One billionaire there who on his own has a fortune of 27 billion dollars,[55] had the great idea of spending millions on the wedding of his child, that he organized high up in the air, in a chartered big jumbo, with hundreds of invitees he paid for! That is how he decided to exhibit his wealth. Little did he recognize that low down on earth, in his own country, millions are struggling for a morsel of food, living in slums and neglected villages that need support. Had the billionaire started from scratch and studied Gandhi's philosophy, this would not have happened.

Pleasure without Conscience

It is natural for persons to enjoy the pleasures that Nature provides. Pleasure that is linked with our five senses is often distinct from happiness. Happiness has a spiritual component that is superior. We are taught to consider our senses like the horses of a chariot, and to control these senses. When let loose, the senses overpower us and pleasures end up in misery. Pleasure without conscience is similar in its effects. That is why Gandhi who was a strong proponent of 'Bramhacharia' or control over our senses, practiced the discipline in his own life, and this is probably what gave him the soul-force to fight for justice in spite of his weak physique. The 'half-naked fakir' as Churchill called him, had the inner strength to pull down the British empire!

Knowledge without Character

This is something we see daily in our environment. Knowledge is power but a power that can destroy when the element of character is not inherent. Knowledge without character is akin to an explosive that can be used for destroying humanity, but combined with wisdom and character, it can enrich humanity. Character is the result of upbringing, while knowledge is the result of instruction that we acquire through schooling and from our parents. Often our schooling unfortunately does not educate the child to develop a deep sense of values. Passing the present system of examinations, getting into a highly paid job, is the result of the knowledge we acquire in schools and colleges. But character is essential to fulfill our roles in life with righteousness. Otherwise we end up with the likes of those responsible for the current global financial crisis!

En passant, I wish to point out that this is what we are imparting through our 'Sukhi Parivaar, or Happy Family' program. Parents have as much if not more responsibility in educating their children than our institutions.

Commerce without Morality

Commerce is an essential component of our civilization. Over the ages commerce has helped nations to interchange goods and the transmission of cultures, and bring humanity closer. When commerce has as objective only the maximization of profits and the accumulation of material wealth, it lacks the element of morality. People are inclined to use any means to achieve their ends. And commerce then becomes a bane for humanity.

We often see people lying from morning till evening, portraying their wares with exaggerated values, claiming above normal profits for the goods and services, reaping windfall gains, and then praying God for forgiving their sins. To some, lying is a common practice in commerce. To others, exacting exorbitant profits, fooling the people, is acceptable practice. When morality is bypassed, how can we expect sins to be forgiven? The law of Karma, or the scientific Law of Action and Reaction, invariably applies. And what will be the use of the wealth accumulated? Gandhi came from a business family, but his vision of human progress was different. He strove to cultivate righteousness in himself and in others, with a high sense of morality at the base. It is necessary for all to read his book: 'My experiments with truth.'

Science without Humanity

Science that is knowledge acquired through observation and measurements, in itself is harmless, innocuous. But the use we make of this knowledge can be often questioned. History is full of cases where science has been badly used for inhuman activities. This is where modern scientists have erred immensely!

These days we see the impact of the abuse made of natural resources and the type of polluting technologies that have been applied. I refer to the earlier paragraphs on global warming and climate changes. The preservation of environment has become a critical issue for all countries. In all these activities science has been used without humanity. When Gandhi proposed a development in tune with nature, he was far ahead of his times! That is why we are now proposing a new type of science and technology, one which is humane.[56] The explosion of the first atomic bomb in Hiroshima in 1945, shook the world, and awakened a consciousness about the negative potential of science. Albert Einstein[57] had seen this potential in his formula $E=MC^2$, and had been very much influenced by the philosophy of Mahatma Gandhi. Most of you would remember his famous statement in praise of the Mahatma on his seventieth birthday: '*Generations to come, it may be, will scarce believe that such a one as this, ever in flesh and blood, walked this earth!*'

Courses and textbooks on science rarely refer to humanity or humanism. We end up with bright professionals who often lack the basics of humanism, and whose dealings are centered on the accumulation of material benefits. With the result that we get a distorted social and economic development, and real happiness keeps running away!

Worship without Sacrifice

For most people, the worship of God with faith and conviction does not usually take place when all is well. It is mainly when problems arise and hope in human intervention diminishes that one turns to Him! But if this worship is without sacrifice, a sacrifice that involves depriving oneself of so many enjoyments and goodies, the worship may not be fruitful. The Mahatma may have noted the showy parades of people participating in religious pilgrimages, often wasting much resource, but with little spirit of sacrifice. Fasting, penance, and self-purification form integral parts of worship. The spirit of sacrifice is the basis of any good activity.

Popular religion has become a pageantry of rites and rituals wherein the real spirit of sacrifice is often absent. The form dominates the essence. No wonder the thinking mind shuns such pageantry. Every action of Gandhi was an act of sacrifice, and it is this that gave him the inner strength to move onwards, in spite of the worst odds on his way. And success was assured. This is what we have to follow today.

Conclusion

Today's global problems of increasing pollution of the environment, unbridled consumerism with gobbling of energy resources and unethical lifestyles, climate change with all its harmful impact of mankind, and growing unemployment caused by the spirit of greed that has led to a global financial crisis are scourges that need a new vision of development. There is no day that passes when there is no war in one place or another on this planet. Mahatma Gandhi's philosophy of life and development can make a signal change to the solution of the problems, provided we know about it, interiorize it and adopt it as a way of life. This will necessitate a change in our lifestyles, a change in our vision. A serious reassessment of our development policies is needed, and we all have a role in this venture, young and old. I appeal especially to our young people here to do this by studying the life and works of Mahatma Gandhi. Just go on the internet, and you can google out the wisdom inherent in this philosophy. Your future is at stake, and no other person than yourself can take control of this future! The ball is in your court!

As Gandhiji said:

'Be the change you wish to see !'

References

[1] 'What Money Can't Buy.' Susan E Mayer, University of Chicago, in 'Limits of Policy' David Brooks, New York Times, May 4, 2010.

[2] Story adapted from Hitopadesh, a series of old Indian fables full of morals. The Hitopadesha, translated by Sir Edwin Arnold, www.columbia.edu/itc/..../hitopadesha_arnold

[3] http://www.asiaone.com/News/AsiaOne%2BNews/Singapore/Story/A1Story20090805-159177.html.

[4] Sudan ex-slaves, swapping school for bread: http://news.bbc.co.uk/2/hi/africa/8647791.stm.

[5] 'A New Development Paradigm, Science and Technology and Economic Theories' by Author, published in *The Journal of Solidarity, Sustainability and Non-Violence*, Vol. 5, No. 4, April 2009, Luis T. Gutierez, Editor.

[6] Schumacher, E.F., 'Small is Beautiful: Economics as if People mattered.' 1973.

[7] 'Suicide in Heaven', *Tony Smart, Le Matinal*, 17.05.10.

[8] Agence France Presse, Tokyo, 'Monster parents plague Japan's schools', Le Matinal, 25.3.10, Mauritius.

[9] COP 15, Copenhagen United Nations Conference on Climate Change, 7–18 December 2009.

[10] Agence France Presse, Tokyo, 19 May 2010, reproduced in Le Matinal, Mauritius, 20.5.10, Port Louis.

[11] http://news.bbc.co.uk/2/hi/europe/8671632.stm.EU Finance Ministers Agree.12.05.10.

[12] http://www.bbc.co.uk/news/business-10656699.

[13] Gerald Edelman, Nobel Prize Winner, 'Neural Darwinism' 1987, The theory of Neuronal Group Selection, New York. The Mindful Brain (MIT) Press, 1978.

[14] Verny, Thomas R., Secret life of unborn child, www.amazon.com/Secret-Life-Unborn-Child-Prepare/dp/0440505658/ref.

[15] Shenk, David, 'The Genius in All of Us', http://www.bbc.co.uk/news/magazine-12140064, 13.01.11.

[16] Erikson, Erik H., http://www.learningplaceonline.com/stages/organize/Erikson.htm

[17] Albert Schweitzer, Memories of Childhood and Youth, p. 99. Albert Schweitzer quotes.

[18] With modern educational system, this stage is rare, but is maintained amongst orthodox Hindus who often follow the Gurukul system of education where children spend years studying under dedicated teachers called 'gurus'.

[19] 'Parenting across the life span, biosocial dimensions' Edited by Jeanne Altman, Alice S. Rossi, Lonnie r Sherrod, 1987, Aldine de Gruyter Publications, Hawthorn, New York.

[20] For a detailed account of 'global warming and financial crisis', see Chapter 10, 'An encounter with parents.'

[21] Paula Spenser: Lessons from the Obamas. Readers Digest, June 2009, http://www.rd-india.com

[22] United Nations, Copenhagen Accord, 2009.

[23] Suffering the science, climate change, people and poverty, Oxfam 2009.

[24] Ageing and development, May 2010.

[25] www.epcc.pref.osaka.jp/apec/eng/earth/global_warming/dounaru.html.

[26] Galbraith, John Kenneth (1908–2006), Canadian-American, 'The Affluent Society', 1958, Wikipedia.

[27] Shiva, Vandana: 'Time to end war against the earth', Outlook India.com, Nov. 11, 2010.

[28] Maharshi Swami Dayanand Saraswati, Founder of the Arya Samaj, a reform movement.

[29] Rene Descartes: www.basicfamouspeople.com/index.php?aid=296.

[30] Mahatma Gandhi Memorial Lecture, Mahatma Gandhi Institute 4th Oct. 2010, Moka.

[31] Diener, E., Emmons, R.A., Larsen, R.J. and Griffin, S., "The satisfaction with life scale.", *Journal of Personality Assessment,* Vol. XLIX, No. 1, 1985.

[32] Easterlin, R.E., *The reluctant Economist, Perspectives on economics, economic history and demography,* Cambridge University Press, 2004.

[33] www.grossnationalhappiness.com.

[34] www.idrc.ca/en/ev-61364-201-1-DO_TOPIC.html.

[35] http:/www.scientificamerican.com/article.cfm?id=the-science-of-lasting-happiness.

[36] Watson, James and Crick, Fancis, http://profiles.nlm.nih.gov/SC/Views/Exhibit.

[37] Human Genome project, http://www.familyhelix.com/articles/human genome.

[38] Tolstoy, by Henri Troyat: 'Arbiter of Peace' and School master. Amazon Books.

[39] www.gandhiserve.org/information/.../brief_philosophy.html.

[40] Indo-Asian News Service, Washington, " Mrs 'O', How does your garden grow?", reproduced in Le Matinal, 4th November. 2010, Mauritius.

[41] Sir Edouard Lim Fat, 'From Vision to Miracle' July 2010, Mauritius. ISBN: 978-99903-22-28-6.

[42] http://www.huxley.net/bnw (Aldous Huxley (1894–1963).

[43] Morgan, Garreth, Technology Reporter, BBC 28.12.10, The Living Earth Simulator, www.bbc.co.uk/news/technology-12012082.

[44] CERN, Large Hadron Collider particle accelerator, public.web.cern.ch/public/en/lhc/lhc

[45] Thaler, Richard and Cass Sunstein, R., 'The Nudge', Improving Decisions about Health, Wealth and Happiness, 2008, Amazon.com.

[46] www.sukhiparivaar.org.

[47] Jugessur, S., E-Journal of solidarity, sustainability and non-violence, http://pelicanweb.org/solisustv05no4page2jugessur.htm.

[48] www.un.org/ecosocdev/..../202-combating-inequality.htm.

[49] Al Gore Nobel Lecture, Oslo, 10 Dec. 2007, http://nobelprize.org.

[50] Smith, Adam ... www.investopedia.com.

[51] Schumacher, Ernst Fredrick, en.wikipedia.org/wiki/Small_Is_Beautiful.

[52] Sarvodaya Movement in India, www.idc.nl/pdf/275_brochure.pdf.

[53] Gandhi, Mahatma, Pictorial Bibliography by Dr. John Mott, Gram Udyog Patrika, 1937.

[54] Heredin, Rudolf C., Economic and Policy weekly, 12.6.99.

[55] Matinal, Le: L'Inde compte un nombre record de milliardaires. Friday 1st October 2010, Mauritius.

[56] Jugessur, S., 'Science Based Development, Policy Issues', ELP Publications, Mauritius 2008.

[57] Einstein, A., www.spaceandmotion.com/Albert Einstein quotes.htm.

Index